Emergency
Preparedness
and Off-Grid
Communication

Emergency
Preparedness
and Off-Grid
Communication

Praying Medic

dhayesMEDIA

DHayes Media LLC, 137 East Elliot Road, #2292, Gilbert, AZ 85299

This book and other DHayes Media titles can be found at: DHayes Media.com Available at Amazon.com and other retail outlets.

For more information visit our website at www.dhayesmedia.com or email us at dave@dhayesmedia.com

ISBN-13: 979-8-9885112-6-7 (DHayes Media)

Printed in the U.S.A.

asset or liability?

Table of Contents

Problems

Introduction

IN 2023, NEWS OUTLETS HAVE frequently published stories warning about the possibility of catastrophic events happening around the globe. Some articles warn of cyber attacks. Others warn of disastrous solar storms. Many speculate about the threat of power outages and nuclear war. Here are just a few headlines from November and December of 2023. Are citizens of our modern world prepared for these possibilities?

As the Israel-Hamas War Governs the World's Attention, Iran Is Quietly Marching Towards Nuclear Breakout
~Time (12/9/23)

China's cyber army is invading critical U.S. services
~Washington Post (12/11/23)

Iran-linked cyberattacks threaten U.S. water, heath care and energy sectors
~NPR (12/2/23)

Don't panic but... Brits should stock up on candles and battery-powered radios in case a power meltdown cripples digital gadgets, Deputy Prime Minister Oliver Dowden warns
~Daily Mail (12/4/23)

UK at high risk of 'catastrophic ransomware attack,' report says
The Guardian (12/12/23)

Earth will be bombarded by intense solar storms next year: Scientists predict we'll reach 'solar maximum' in 2024 - with flares strong enough to cripple the world's internet for weeks
~Daily Mail (11/29/23)

Doomsday clock warns world of catastrophe in 2024
~Jerusalem Post (12/4/23)

My personal interest in emergency preparedness began in 1995, when I moved to Washington State and took a job as a firefighter paramedic with a small municipal fire department. Due to its close proximity to many geologic faults, Western Washington experiences frequent earthquakes. One fault in particular has worried geologists. The Cascadia subduction zone fault that runs along the Washington and Oregon coastline is not your garden-variety crack in the earth's crust. The fault is formed where the Pacific and North American tectonic plates meet. Historical records show that every few hundred years, this fault is the site of earthquakes that suddenly lower the entire western coast of North America by several feet. Geologists generally believe another such earthquake is overdue.

Western Washington also sees frequent windstorms that knock down power lines, which can leave people without electricity for weeks until the lines are repaired. My work with the fire department offered me an opportunity to teach community preparedness with a focus on preparing for large earthquakes and power outages.

Note that my preparedness focused on two threats. One of those threats—a massive earthquake—was a rare occurrence, but it was potentially life-altering if it happened. The other risk—a power outage—was not life-threatening, but it was a common, well-known issue. I did not prepare for hurricanes or tornadoes because they were extremely unlikely to happen where I lived. I prepared for the kind of events that would be reasonably expected to occur in Western Washington.

Minor earthquakes are common in Western Washington, but a quake of 8.0 magnitude could leave millions of people homeless. To prepare for that possibility, I put together a bug-out bag for each member of my family, which included a tent, sleeping bag, cook stove, bottled water, flashlight, matches, food, and a few other items. The bug-out bag was to be used to get each of us by for a few days if an earthquake destroyed our house. I also bought a generator and some extension cords and stored a couple of cans of gasoline in my garage to prepare for the power outages. The bug-out bags were never needed, but I used the generator regularly. These simple measures addressed the two main threats my family faced when I lived in Washington.

And that is the main goal of preparedness. We can't prepare for every possible emergency—and we don't have to. The first step in preparedness is identifying the specific threats you ought to prepare for, keeping in mind that we only need to prepare for the most *serious* and the most *likely* scenarios that could cause us hardship. It's foolish to prepare for hurricanes if you live in Montana. For the most part, threats to our way of life are specific to where we live. Having said that, we should also prepare for threats that are national or global in scope. This book discusses ways to prepare for such threats.

Some people avoid preparing for disasters because they don't know what to prepare for. Feeling overwhelmed, they choose to avoid the issue altogether. The information provided in this book will show you that you don't need to prepare for every possible crisis. You only need to prepare for the one that is the most likely to happen to you and the one that has the most potential to alter your way of life. We'll examine the risk profiles of potential disasters and ask questions to help determine if each is a realistic threat to you.

Some people avoid the issue of preparedness because they don't have the money required to buy the things they believe they might need. If this describes you, take heart. There are some things you can do to prepare that cost little or nothing except some basic skills and creative thinking.

For twelve years, God has warned me about a variety of potential future crises. (I use the word "potential" because it is difficult to speak with absolute certainty when dealing with prophetic revelation—matters to do with the future.) I've received dreams warning of widespread power outages, communication disruptions, food shortages, economic collapse, and one dream hinting at nuclear war. It would be negligent of me not to share these warnings with others, along with tips about preparing for them. My goal with this book is to provide common-sense preparations that can be made for specific events that I believe we may see in the near future.

1

Mental Preparedness

FOR PREPAREDNESS TO BE SUCCESSFUL, it must become a lifestyle and not just an occasional thing you think about a few times a year. It's a mindset that should affect the decisions you make on a daily basis. How well-prepared you are for a crisis will depend on the decisions you've made and the habits you've developed over the previous years. Habits that will help you in a crisis are developed during times of peace.

Half the battle of getting ready for the unexpected is mental preparedness. Many people first consider preparing for a crisis after being made aware of a potential future problem. Concerned that they might be caught off guard, they wonder if they should take steps to deal with the potential problem. Concern can motivate us, but excessive worry can interfere with rational thought. Preparedness is best done with a clear mind and a sober, realistic outlook. A primary goal is to recognize and address legitimate problems while discarding unrealistic concerns that do not require preparedness.

Ask any member of a military special operations team what the key is to surviving adverse conditions and achieving difficult goals, and they'll tell you that nothing they do is possible without proper mental preparedness. You can have the best gear and years of training in how to use it, but without the right mindset, you will not use your equipment effectively.

With our minds focused on the issues of daily life, many of us are unaware of the dangers that surround us. When faced with a sudden threat, we go from a mental state of unawareness to a state of panic in a matter of seconds. When our mind is filled with fear, we can't think rationally. We make errors in judgment or freeze when we should be reacting to a threat. *Situational awareness* is our ability to recognize and respond to threats.

Jeff Cooper developed a system that describes the different levels of situational awareness based on color codes. Cooper's color codes are divided into five categories: white, yellow, orange, red, and black. Level white is when you're not aware of what is going on around you. You're unaware of potential threats and unprepared for an assault. In condition yellow, you're aware of your surroundings—prepared but relaxed. In level orange, you've recognized a possible threat and are prepared to act on it. In level red, you've engaged a threat, and your focus is on dealing with it. While focusing on the immediate threat, a secondary focus is on other possible dangers and potential help from strangers, friends, or law enforcement. In condition black, you panic, freeze, and shut down. This is the worst possible state. Condition yellow is where we should be most of the time. Our eyes are scanning the environment, looking for potential threats, but we're physically relaxed. Maintaining proper awareness is helpful during times of peace, but it's critical during a crisis.

Adverse environments and difficult tasks present physical and mental problems that can overwhelm us. No one thinks of giving up when life is easy, but when adversity comes, we face the temptation to quit. When times are hard, the thought of giving up must be opposed by a reason to keep going. If the reason to persevere is stronger than the reason to quit, one will generally continue fighting. Before beginning a difficult pursuit, it helps to find a compelling reason to see the task through to its completion.

What is your reason for reading this book? Why do you want to prepare for a potential disaster?

Your motivation may be as simple as wanting to be prepared for a power outage caused by a hurricane. Some have pragmatic reasons for prepping, but others have ideological reasons. Perhaps you value liberty above all else and feel a need to fight against the forces of tyranny. Maybe you desire to pass along to your grandchildren the values and lessons you've learned in life. Whatever your motivation is, think about it every day during a crisis. Continually reminding yourself why you are doing what you are doing will drive out the temptation to quit when times are hard. Mental preparedness is the most important asset you have. Nothing can force you to quit if you're mentally prepared for adversity.

2

What Should I Prepare For?

IT'S A WASTE OF TIME and resources to prepare for an event that will never happen to you. Likewise, there's little point in preparing for an event that will have little impact on your way of life. To prepare for potential disasters, you need to identify the ones that are the most likely to happen and the ones that will have the greatest impact. In this chapter, we'll assess the likelihood that certain disasters might occur to you and their probable impact. This will help determine which ones are worth preparing for. In assessing risk, we need to look at what facts are known to experts in these areas. Most of the facts that experts rely on come from analyzing historical trends. Weather and geologic trends tend to be predictable. Past patterns can help predict future events. So, we'll look at past disasters and discuss their likelihood of happening again.

Gathering / Analyzing Data

When evaluating the kinds of threats we're likely to face, we should consider the fact that not every possible threat that comes to our attention is a real threat. Likewise, there may be real threats that we're unaware of. We can take steps to learn which threats are real and which are not. Gathering and discerning the reliability of information is critical to making good decisions.

There are two common mistakes people make when assessing threats. The first is failing to gather enough information. The lazy person doesn't do their homework. Thus, they have no reliable information that can be used to evaluate threats, and they don't know what to prepare for.

The second is information overload. Some people read every article and watch every video they can find on a subject and consider all of it to be valid, when in fact, much of it should be ignored because it's flawed in some way. This person lacks discernment and tends to make decisions that are poorly informed.

If you don't critically evaluate the many pieces of information available, you're likely to become either apathetic or overwhelmed by what you find. A lot of what is available on the internet can be disregarded as hype or fear-mongering.

When I hear about a potential threat, I research the subject using material from different viewpoints. I evaluate the arguments on both sides of the issue and look for logical fallacies and inconsistencies. I note the tone of the presenters. If a presenter is excessively emotional, it can indicate that they're reacting to the issue from their own irrational fear. If the information is presented in a convincing way without contradictions, logical fallacies, and excessive fear, I'll ask God to give me further insights. Generally, when He wants to draw my attention to a particular issue, He'll give me dreams about it. God speaks in many ways. He may choose to inform you through something other than a dream. The key is to be still, and pay attention after asking. Sometimes the answer will come days later.

One factor to consider is the severity of the impact that a threat has. By severity, I mean how much damage a threat poses to your way of life. A windstorm that takes out power lines in a neighborhood for a few days has a much lower severity than one that uproots thousands of trees and leaves a million people without power. Another factor to consider is the frequency of a threat. A storm that happens once every hundred years is less likely to impact us than one that happens every few years. When you combine the severity and frequency of a threat, you begin to build a risk profile, which helps gauge whether it should be included in your preparedness plans.

Wind Storms

Some locations are prone to frequent wind storms. The Puget Sound is one such area and it has a unique set of risks. The region sees frequent storms with wind gusts over 40 MPH, along with heavy rains. Many of the coniferous trees in the area have shallow roots. This leads to large trees being toppled that damage homes and power lines. If home damage and power outages are a concern for you, consider living in an area where these storms seldom happen. If you must live in a region where windstorms are common, preparedness involves having the tools and supplies needed to make home repairs and providing for emergency backup power. (This will be discussed in the "Loss of Power" chapter.)

Tornadoes

Among natural disasters, tornadoes present a unique risk profile. Even though they only last a few minutes, and generally strike rural areas, if you happen to be in the path of one, the devastation can be incredible. While a large tornado can level a small community, they don't cause damage outside of the immediate area where they occur. While the impact of an earthquake or hurricane can be felt for thousands of miles, tornadoes pose a threat to a small geographic area and a few people.

The risk of being caught in a tornado can be calculated with reasonable accuracy. I'm not referring to the actual probability of a particular person being hit by a specific tornado. I'm referring to the overall exposure to the risk of a tornado during a person's lifetime, based on where they live. There are some locations where tornadoes are common, others where they are less common, and many places where they are seldom (or never) seen. You can determine your risk by looking at weather maps showing the historical frequency and severity of tornadoes in your area.

If tornadoes are a concern for you, consider living in a place where they seldom occur. If you must live in a place where tornadoes occur frequently, preparedness is aimed at not getting yourself killed. Preventing crop and property damage from a tornado is practically impossible. Serious preppers usually avoid living in these danger zones. People who live in tornado country usually have cellars and basements for shelter. If you need to build a shelter as a safe place to hide from a tornado, make it large enough for food and other things you may want to store up for possible long-term crises as well.

Hurricanes

Hurricanes, like tornadoes, have a risk profile that can be easily determined. Hurricanes form over warm bodies of water in the tropics. They only present a threat once they move toward land. Because they move slowly, their approach can be anticipated by weather forecasters. Historical records provide accurate information about the likelihood of a hurricane happening in a particular area. Warnings are usually posted days in advance of a hurricane making landfall, and wise people leave the area before it hits. Hurricanes present a couple of unique problems. They often have sustained winds that exceed 100 miles per hour. These winds can topple trees and power lines, making life miserable in the aftermath. Hurricanes also bring heavy rains and a wall of water known as a storm surge. A storm surge is a sustained wave of water that temporarily raises the level at which water meets land, creating flooding.

From a strategic perspective, coastal areas prone to hurricanes are a poor choice for preppers because they're subject to frequent, violent storms that threaten safety. You can choose to live in one of these areas, but you must do so knowing that you're putting yourself in harm's way.

If you must live in an area prone to hurricanes, prepping is generally aimed at getting you through the week or two of crisis that follows a major storm. Your goals would be to obtain backup sources of power, reserves of food and water, and anything else you might need to sustain you and your family during a short-term crisis.

In a crisis where your home is no longer livable, seek temporary shelter at a friend or relative's home. (You will see a recurring theme in this book that stresses the importance of building relationships and community.) If no other option is available, government agencies like FEMA usually have temporary shelters set up where food and water are provided.

Earthquakes

The Pacific coast of North America is part of a geologic phenomenon known as "the Ring of Fire." The name comes from the fact that there is a string of active volcanoes along this line where continental tectonic plates meet. These areas are prone to both severe earthquakes and volcanic activity. I lived in the Pacific Northwest for 16 years, and in that time, I walked on ground that regularly quaked. I felt three of these earthquakes, though many more happened which I did not feel. Two quakes were minor, causing only a gentle sensation of swaying back and forth. The third was more violent, causing more than 400 injuries and some damage to buildings that were not strengthened to withstand a strong quake.

Earthquake activity along the Ring of Fire is predictable. There are frequent small quakes that happen by the hundreds every day. These quakes cannot be felt. There are less frequent quakes that are a bit larger in size and are felt only if you're near the epicenter. There are occasional major quakes every few months, larger ones every few years, and mega quakes once every three or four hundred years.

By understanding the frequency and severity of earthquakes, you can make an informed decision about whether such a place suits your needs. If you choose to live in a region prone to earthquakes, you can do a few things to minimize your exposure to damage.

One day, a few years after moving to the Northwest, I visited the county assessor's office. The county had maps that showed the geologic composition of the land inside the county borders. The county has several rivers that empty into the Puget Sound. The proximity to a river valley is important when evaluating land and its potential for earthquake-related problems.

Historically, the most likely places to suffer earthquake damage are river valleys. The geologic composition of river valleys includes a lot of sand. When earthquakes hit, the sand combines with water to form a liquefied slurry that shifts quickly, causing buildings to suffer damage, even during quakes that do not affect other areas.

My neighborhood was on an elevated plain 300 feet above sea level, a couple of miles from the Nisqually River valley. The geologic composition was mixed rock that was relatively stable regarding seismic activity. Although our home was shaken hard during the 6.8 Nisqually earthquake in 2001, it survived without so much as a crack in the sheet rock, due to how it was built. New homes in that region must be constructed with engineering devices that improve the odds of withstanding a major quake. If you live in an area prone to earthquakes, find out if your home is built to comply with earthquake building codes. It's also a good idea to find out the geologic composition of your property. If you live in or near a river valley, your home is more likely to suffer damage in an earthquake. If that's a concern, you might consider moving to another location. If you must live in such an area, factor into your plans the possibility of having your home severely damaged or destroyed and being forced to move temporarily.

Flooding

Many people desire waterfront property and purchase land with river-front access or a lot near a river or stream. There are many reasons why these locations are appealing to home buyers. Access to fishing and boating are the most obvious reasons, but price is usually a factor as well. While river-front property can be expensive, adjacent land in a river valley is often cheap. And if it's cheap, there's usually a reason why.

One of the major concerns for preppers is access to a reliable water source. Experts agree that access to water is the number one priority for a long-term preparedness plan. Having a piece of land with a stream not only provides a source of water but may provide a source of food if the stream has fish in it. Rivers and streams are a source of water for wildlife. Deer and other wild game will frequently be found near them. If your preparedness plans include hunting wild game, having a piece of land with access to a river or stream makes a lot of sense. But there are downsides to living on a piece of land near a river or stream. We already discussed the issue of seismic instability in river valleys. Flooding is another potential problem.

A tract of land located within the floodplain of a river is a hundred times more likely to be flooded than property a few hundred feet away that lies outside the floodplain. You should do some research on any piece of property you plan to purchase near a river or stream. You'll want to look for any insurance claims involving damages due to flooding. Ask your insurance agent about the risk profile for the piece of land with regard to flooding. If the land lies within the floodplain and there's a chance it could be flooded, the agent should be able to tell you. The likelihood of flooding will determine how much you'll pay to insure it. Weigh the benefits and risks before buying land near a river or stream.

Mudslides

Every year, mudslides kill many people and wash away homes. These disasters always have the same basic profile. They happen in places with steep, hilly terrain, often near the edge of a cliff. And they happen after several days or weeks of unusually heavy rain. Heavy rain and steep terrain are a disaster waiting to happen. When normally dry land is saturated with heavy rain, it turns to a soupy consistency, and it can't hold its shape. If the land happens to be high up on a hillside, gravity will pull it downward like a blob of pudding. Anything that was built on the piece of land will come down with it.

Understandably, some people want to build homes perched on hilltops and cliffs overlooking a scenic valley or a body of water. The ambiance of these locations is tempting. But homeowners who want to be prepared for the worst-case scenario should carefully consider whether it's worth risking their lives to have a spectacular hilltop or cliff-side view. If the land you're living on is precariously close to the edge of a cliff or a steep hill and your area is prone to even occasionally heavy rain, you might reconsider the location and choose somewhere safer. And if my argument hasn't convinced you, consider this: a safer piece of land will probably cost you much less.

Winter Storms

As with other weather-related disasters, winter storms are a risk that can be predicted accurately. Some areas have blizzards and ice-storms with regularity while others seldom experience them. Winter storms cause several problems. One is the possibility of death from hypothermia. Ice storms can damage trees and cause power outages. Prolonged power outages can put you at risk of freezing to death. Another risk is death or injury from traveling by car or foot in snow and ice.

Most people are aware of the risk of getting in a serious car accident in a winter storm. But few are aware of an even greater danger. Every year, thousands of people die from complications after fracturing their hip in a fall. Consider this hypothetical situation: You slip on a patch of ice and fracture your hip. You go to a hospital to have it surgically repaired, and then go to a rehabilitation facility to learn how to walk again. You develop a post-operative infection and are re-admitted to the hospital. The infection is so severe that multiple courses of antibiotics are required, and despite the treatment, you die from pneumonia. According to the Centers for Disease Control, the fourth leading killer of Americans every year is respiratory infection. Many of those infections develop after surgery.

Areas that are subject to frequent winter storms may not be an ideal place for a prepper. But if you must live in such a location, there are steps you can take to make life less risky. Preparedness involves storing up food so you won't have to leave home during a storm, and having an alternate source of heat in the event that electricity is unavailable or fuel deliveries cannot be made. If your home loses power and your pipes freeze, you may lose access to water, so be sure to have some in storage.

Desert Dangers

Millions of people live in the desert biomes of the Southwestern United States. I happen to be one of them. We don't worry about earthquakes, hurricanes, tornadoes, mudslides, and other natural disasters. They rarely happen here. Prepping in the desert comes with a unique challenge. Phoenix receives less than 10 inches of rain a year. High temperatures average around 102 degrees from June through September. Daily highs can be between 115 and 120 degrees. Groundwater is generally of poor quality, and well-drilling is expensive due to the hardness of the soil. There are few rivers or streams available year-round. Most of the water used for irrigation comes from the Colorado River and is distributed through hundreds of miles of open canals that crisscross the state.

The risks for those who live in the desert are heat related illnesses such as dehydration, heat exhaustion, and heat stroke. In the southwestern U.S., drinkable water is in short supply. Preparation for those who live in hot climates involves storing an emergency supply of water and having backup power for cooling in the event of a power outage.

If you must live in an area prone to disasters, it's worth taking time to learn what they are, how often they occur, and what (if any) methods have been developed to reduce their impact.

3

Without the Rule of Law

IN 2023, VIDEOS APPEARED ON social media showing mobs of people committing acts of retail theft in the cities of Portland, Seattle, New York City, San Fransisco, and Los Angeles. District attorneys in these cities chose not to prosecute many of the perpetrators. In September of 2023, Target announced it would close stores in these cities due to vandalism and theft.

In the summer of 2020, protests broke out across the United States in reaction to the death of George Floyd. The vandalism and looting that occurred between May 26th and June 8th caused between $1 and 2 billion in damages nationwide—the highest recorded damage from civil unrest in U.S. history. Few people were prosecuted for their participation in the riots.

On January 6th, 2021, protests were held at the Capitol building in Washington D.C., in response to the 2020 election. Hundreds of protesters who committed no acts of violence were charged and convicted of felony crimes and given prison sentences. Enrique Tarrio was not in Washington that day, but was convicted of seditious conspiracy and sentenced to 22 years. What are we to make of the fact that one group of people seems to be immune to criminal punishment while another group appears to be unjustly targeted by the government?

On October 4th, 2023, President Joe Biden announced that he was forgiving $9 billion in student loan debt, despite the

U.S. Supreme Court ruling that the President does not have the authority to forgive such debt. Is the executive branch of government above the law?

The rule of law in the U.S.—and other countries around the world—is in trouble. Many people believe we live under a two-tiered system of justice, where one set of laws is enforced upon some people while a different legal standard is applied to others. In September of 2023, United States Attorney General Merrick Garland—the highest law enforcement officer in the land—insisted that there are not two standards of justice in the United States. Garland's defense of the Department of Justice was necessary because he knows the public believes that there are, in fact, two standards of justice.

One danger of imposing unequal application of the law is that those who know they will not be punished will commit more crimes. The safety and security of every citizen is in danger when we live without the rule of law.

Many states have enacted laws prohibiting the possession of certain types of semi-automatic rifles. The U.S. Constitution does not prohibit the ownership of such weapons, but elected leaders have chosen to circumvent the Constitution in pursuit of an agenda. This behavior is dangerous because it tempts normally law-abiding citizens to disregard statutes and regulations, believing the government has overstepped its authority. When the government does not respect the principles upon which the nation was founded, it has gone rogue in the eyes of citizens. When citizens no longer view government as legitimate, society is ripe for civil unrest.

State of Emergency

In times of disaster or civil unrest, a state of emergency is usually declared by a government official. An emergency declaration allows local, state, or federal governments to expand their powers temporarily to deal with a crisis, suspending some civil liberties while avoiding military control. Emergency declarations are common in the U.S. and are easily reversed.

Martial Law

Martial law is the temporary substitution of military authority for the civilian rule of law. It is usually invoked during
war, rebellion, or a large-scale natural disaster. Martial law
is justified when civilian authority has ceased functioning, is
absent, or is deemed ineffective. In the U.S., martial law may be
declared by proclamation of the President or a State governor.
The declaration of martial law suspends all existing civil laws,
civil authority, and the ordinary administration of justice. The
justice system that typically handles issues of criminal and civil
law is replaced with the Uniform Code of Military Justice. When
martial law is declared, civil liberties such as the right to free
assembly, free speech, protection from unreasonable search
and seizure, the right to bear arms, and the right to a speedy
trial may be suspended. Civilians may be arrested for violating curfews or for offenses that would not normally warrant
detention. The authority of martial law does have limitations.
Civilians may not be tried by military tribunals if civilian courts
are available. Nevertheless, concerning legal administration,
a military commander's authority under martial law is virtually
unlimited. Preparation for martial law involves learning what
is considered lawful conduct under these new codes of justice,
and how it differs from the normal lawful conduct.

If martial law is declared where you live, keep yourself
informed about curfews as they're imposed. Stay abreast of
announcements that inform the public about areas where civilians are prohibited, such as government buildings. Know if it
has been declared unlawful to carry a firearm. Be aware if protests have been prohibited, and avoid participating in public
assemblies until they are allowed. In a crisis, this information
should be available through broadcasts on television and radio.
Staying informed about changes in lawful behavior will keep
you out of jail and in your home, where you are safer, and where
you can help your friends and neighbors.

4

Loss of Power

MANY OF THE DEVICES THAT make life convenient are powered by electricity. When power is disrupted, life becomes much more challenging.

Lighting

One of the first concerns when planning for an emergency should be lighting. Before electric lights were invented, people used candles and lamps that burn oil, kerosene, or other flammables. These sources of light will also be handy in an emergency. If you intend to use candles, camp stoves or fuel-powered lanterns in a crisis, be sure to purchase an ample supply of strike-anywhere matches or butane lighters. Battery-powered flashlights and lanterns are more convenient, and because there is little risk of starting a fire with them, they're safer.

Chemical lights (glow sticks) are disposable plastic tubes that emit colored light. They don't require fuel or batteries and they're portable. Once activated, they can last for 24 hours or more (depending on the brand), which you should consider before using. If you only need light for a few minutes, a flashlight may be a better option.

I keep a battery-powered headlamp in my kitchen for trips outside at night. These handy little lights have adjustable straps to keep them on your head. Imagine making a trip to the bathroom in the middle of the night when there is no power, and you'll appreciate why having one of these for each person in your home is a good idea. Try to standardize your lighting equipment around one or two common battery sizes to eliminate the need to buy multiple types of batteries. Single use batteries are fine for seldom used items. For items that are used frequently, consider using rechargeable batteries.

In a crisis, it's wise to reduce energy consumption. A floor lamp with a 60 watt incandescent bulb consumes ten times as much power as a 6 watt LED bulb that puts out comparable illumination. A home that uses LED bulbs can be lit with a fraction of the power needed to illuminate one with incandescent bulbs.

Gas Appliances

When a power grid suffers a service disruption, the local supply of natural gas is not affected in most cases. Many gas companies have generators powered by natural gas that will keep gas distribution lines supplied. But even if natural gas is available, some gas appliances will not work. When electric power is disrupted, a gas *stove top* will work because it can be lit with a match when the electric pilot light loses power. However, most modern gas *ovens* will be unusable in a power outage. Older ovens allowed users to access the pilot light, but modern gas ovens may not allow such access due to safety features. If the electric pilot light is inoperable, there won't be a safe and easy option for lighting it manually.

How about your gas furnace? A gas furnace also has an electric pilot light that cannot be lit manually and requires a thermostat and fan powered by electricity. Most gas water heaters will not work in a blackout as the pilot light and thermostat require electric power. Most gas fireplaces can be lit with a match when the pilot light loses power.

Cooking

An alternative to cooking on a conventional stove top is to use an electric hot plate plugged into a generator. Another option is a propane-powered camping stove, which are available with one or two burners. A charcoal, natural gas, propane grill or fire pit are other alternatives.

Heating and Cooling

An electric space heater can provide heat in an emergency when powered by a generator. (Generators will be discussed shortly.) Kerosene space heaters can be used intermittently indoors, but caution should be used as they create hazardous fumes like carbon monoxide. Always use in a ventilated area.

If you need air conditioning in a crisis but can't or don't want to use a window air conditioner, Honeywell makes a line of portable air conditioners that can be powered by a generator. Alternatively, you might consider purchasing a few electric fans and powering them with a solar or gas powered generator.

Conserving Energy

Coffee makers, blenders, radios, hair dryers, and other small household appliances can be powered by a small generator. Larger generators can power larger appliances. Keep in mind that the more energy an appliance requires, the less power is left for other appliances. One way to maximize your use of emergency power is to consider hand washing your clothes and hanging them on a line to dry (weather permitting) instead of using an electric washer and dryer. A standard clothesline can be tied between supports in your yard, or you can use paracord. Alternatively, you can purchase a clothes drying rack and hang your wet clothes up to dry inside.

A compromise is to use a small portable washing machine designed for use in apartments. They use a fraction of the electricity and water of a conventional washing machine. They're easy to carry, and can be used outside or in a bathtub. Compact washing machines are filled with a few gallons of water from a hose or bucket, and the water is drained wherever it's convenient. Because they can be used outside, a solar generator can be recharged as it provides power to the washing machine.

TIP: A small washing machine requires a fraction of the soap needed for a regular-sized one.

Generators

During a power outage, most people rely on a generator to supply needed electricity. Propane, natural gas, and gasoline-powered generators are sources of electricity, and they come in different sizes. Some generators are permanently installed while others are portable. Some are designed to power a few small appliances. Others can power an entire home. Nearly all generators provide power to appliances that require 120 volts. Some can power appliances that require 220 volts. Calculate the voltage and wattage of the items you plan to power with any generator. **TIP:** Determining the power requirements of your refrigerator is a good first step in developing your emergency plan. This information can usually be found on a label somewhere on the appliance.

Generators that run on gasoline, propane, or natural gas must be used outdoors to prevent asphyxiation. Generally, the appliances that need power are indoors, so extension cords will be required. Make sure you have the needed adapters and extension cords for the devices you intend to power with a generator. When considering whether to use a generator during times of societal unrest, be aware that the noise of a generator may draw the attention of thieves looking for someone with food and other items they can steal. A well-lit house in the middle of a row of darkened homes is a sign to criminals that you're more prepared than your neighbors. This could make you a target for burglars. In a hostile environment, be as unnoticeable as possible. If you must use lights at night, do so discretely and make as little noise as possible.

When evaluating generators, consider fuel availability. Propane can be stored for years without degradation, but gasoline has a shelf life of about a year, which can be extended by adding a stabilizer. Gasoline may become expensive or unavailable in a crisis. Natural gas should be available during a power outage.

Which Type of Generator?

Portable solar panels and solar generators can provide power to electronic devices and appliances virtually anywhere. They're quiet, which gives them an advantage over fuel-powered generators. Solar panels are deployed outside where sunlight is available. Small solar panels usually have a charge controller that allows them to power small electronic devices. Larger solar panels can be used to charge a solar generator that has a bank of batteries and an inverter. Once charged, the solar generator can be brought inside to provide power either by directly plugging devices into it or by using extension cords. Multiple solar panels can be connected to provide more power to charge a generator. The drawback of solar power is that it is limited by the availability of sunshine. While it may be an excellent option for those living in states like Arizona and Florida, it would not be a wise option for someone living in Seattle, where sunshine is scarce.

If you want to provide power to a variety of rooms and appliances, it can be done, but there are costs and limitations. An assessment should be made to determine which of your electric appliances and lights are essential during a crisis and which are not. Do you need heating or air conditioning? Do you have a well with an electric pump? Can you get by without a hair dryer and curling iron? Can you boil water and pour it into a coffee filter instead of using an electric coffeemaker? What do you need, and what can you live without temporarily? Make a list of what appliances are essential and develop a plan to provide power for these items.

Once you've determined what items require power, find out the power consumption of each item in watts. Total up the number of watts you'll need to generate and use that number as a guide for building a backup power plan.

If you only want to provide power to a couple of appliances at a time, a 2,000 watt generator is an inexpensive option. If you want to provide power to more appliances, the typical 2,000-square-foot home can be powered by a generator that produces between 7,000 and 10,000 watts.

A whole-house generator can be installed by a licensed electrician. They're often installed with a switch that starts the generator automatically when electric service is disrupted. A less expensive option is to use a generator that is manually connected to your home's breaker panel. If you'd like to consider this option, here's how it is usually done:

You hire a licensed electrician to install a receptacle outside your house that connects to your generator using a cable. The receptacle is wired to your breaker panel. The cable transfers power from your fixed or portable generator to your home's breaker panel via the receptacle.

It is unsafe and illegal to generate your own power and send it into the power grid without authorization. Doing so could cause injury or death to someone working on a power line they believe is not energized. So, a device called an interlock is installed on your home's breaker panel. The interlock allows only one source of power to be used at a time. Along with the interlock, a new breaker is installed that brings power from the generator to the breaker panel.

When the generator is to be used, the interlock requires the main breaker switch to be turned off. This prevents electricity from the power grid from coming into the breaker panel, and it prevents power from the generator from being sent into the power grid. Once the main breaker has been turned off, the new breaker that energizes the panel with power from the generator can be turned on.

Before the generator is started, all switches in the breaker panel should be in the off position. Once the generator is running, turn on the breaker switch that brings power to the panel from the generator. Next, you will choose which devices in your home will receive power and turn on the breaker switches that feed them.

If you don't need the entire home to be powered, a smaller output generator can be used. **NOTE:** Consult an electrician to find out if a soft start mechanism must be installed on your AC unit for it to work properly with your generator. Get an estimate of the costs for parts and labor before purchasing any equipment. Once installed, be sure to test the system ahead of an actual emergency.

Permanent Solar Panels

Solar power is growing in popularity and many people have bought or leased solar panels that provide power to their homes. There are three ways to utilize power from permanently installed solar panels. The first option is to connect them to an existing power grid. With this option the home is powered by electricity from the power grid. Energy produced by the solar panels is sent to the grid. The power produced by the solar panels is compared to the power used by the home. Owners are usually given a rebate for any excess power they provide above the power they use.

As previously mentioned, a power source can't send electricity into the grid while it is not energized without putting power company workers at risk. When the local power grid goes down, grid-tied solar panels are required to shut down, too. I've brought this up because some homeowners mistakenly believe their grid-tied solar panels will provide power to their homes if the local power grid goes down. This assumption is incorrect. If your local power grid goes down, your grid-tied solar panels will be unusable (unless you've installed a hybrid system, which is discussed below).

The second option is to use solar panels in an off-grid configuration. With this arrangement, permanently mounted solar panels send power to a bank of batteries. Solar panels generate DC current, which can be stored in batteries. Household appliances require AC current. Thus, an inverter is used to change the DC current to AC current. A home that has off-grid solar panels is not connected to the power grid.

The third option is a hybrid. With this setup, electricity from the power grid can power the home but it can also receive power from solar panels when the grid goes down. This option requires a special inverter (some systems use two inverters) to handle power from the grid and from a bank of batteries that are charged by solar panels. This option is the most expensive in terms of equipment.

If you need information about setting up a solar power system, contact a licensed electrician and a reputable company that sells solar panels and accessories. They'll be able to help you design a system that meets your needs and provide a cost estimate.

5

How Reliable is the Internet?

DURING THE COVID PANDEMIC OF 2020, many scientific experts had their social media posts removed and their accounts suspended because they dared to challenge the mainstream narrative about the treatment of covid. Dozens of my friends and I had our YouTube accounts suspended on October 15, 2020, the day after the *New York Post* published its bombshell report revealing incriminating evidence found on a laptop belonging to President Joe Biden's son Hunter. It was later learned that elected officials and representatives of government agencies pressured social media platforms to take such action. It is unlawful (in the U.S.) for the government to interfere with first amendment protected speech, so those who wanted to censor certain view-points did it through third parties that had no such restrictions. In the landmark case Missouri v Biden, a federal judge issued a ruling prohibiting government agencies from pressuring social media companies to take action against users who post material protected by the first amendment.

These actions reveal a desire by those in power to silence anyone who opposes them. The need to silence an opponent arises from a desire to remain in power. It is my view that the political establishment will do virtually anything to maintain its grip on power. I believe the regime would sabotage social media platforms and email services, and render the internet itself unusable if that is what it took to avoid being removed from power.

Jen Easterly, the Director of CISA (the U.S. government's cyber security agency), released statements in 2023 warning that both Russia and China are planning cyber attacks against the United States. The warning about China was particularly dire, saying that Chinese threat actors had been making preparations to attack U.S. critical infrastructure. Easterly said, "I hope that people are taking seriously a pretty stark warning about the potential for China to use their very formidable capabilities in the event of a conflict in the Taiwan straits to go after our critical infrastructure."

Easterly suggests that a foreign nation will strike the U.S. critical infrastructure as part of an escalating conflict that could lead to war. The September 11, 2001, World Trade Center disaster became the pretext for war in Afghanistan. It also led to the passage of the Patriot Act—a legislative package that neutralized the 4th amendment prohibition against unlawful search and seizure. A single incident allowed the administrative state to legitimize a new war and greatly enhance its ability to spy on citizens illegally. I suspect Easterly's warning about a cyber attack is the regime's way of creating a public narrative in advance of future incidents that will render our current means of communication useless. If, as Easterly predicts, a large-scale cyber attack occurs, it will no doubt adversely affect internet and cell phone communications.

Loss of Internet

I grew up in the 1960s, long before smartphones and the internet were part of our culture. Life was simpler then. We communicated primarily by telephone and letters sent through the postal service. I bring this up only to remind readers that although the internet plays a vital role in most people's lives, we got by for thousands of years without it.

That said, the internet today is the lifeblood of financial, governmental, commercial, infrastructural, medical, social, and military services. A sustained loss of service would be disastrous for world commerce and banking. Global transportation is coordinated via the internet. A disruption of communication between airport terminals and airplanes, ships and shipyards, buses, trains, and commercial trucking companies and vendors would bring these services to a screeching halt, at least temporarily. Infrastructurally, an internet outage could cause a loss of electrical power, television, and even water distribution. The medical industry relies heavily on the internet to store the information needed to diagnose and treat patients.

Although a small segment of the population does not rely on the internet, billions of people would lose the way they receive information and communicate with friends and family. The world wide web is hard-wired into our lives. Many people are unable to read a map. They rely exclusively on navigation apps. The loss of phone and internet service would leave them without the ability to get to destinations other than routes to locations they have memorized. Even the post office, which, decades ago, delivered letters without the internet, might not be able to do so efficiently today.

For more than 100 years, people relied on the telephone to stay in touch with loved ones. Most modern landline phones today are not connected by copper wires as they were years ago. Telecom companies today generally send voice messages over the internet. From a communications perspective, a loss of the internet would not set us back 50 years to a time before the web existed. It could set us back 100 years to a time before the telephone was widely used. Loss of access to cell phone and internet service would create many problems. That is why a large portion of this book is devoted to exploring alternate means of communication. **TIP:** Keep in a safe place a printed list of important contacts that includes physical street addresses in case you need to navigate to a particular residence or mail someone a letter when the internet is not available.

6

Traveling During a Crisis

FOR THOUSANDS OF YEARS, MANKIND relied on a set of tools to help find a path to a desired location. Today, many people would not be able to find a street address on the other side of town without a navigation app on their mobile device. When phone and internet service is unavailable, it's critical to know how to navigate using other methods.

The science of navigation is built on the idea that if one finds a known direction, one can assign other directions that exist in fixed relationships to it. Basic navigation begins with knowing one direction. If you face the sun in the early morning, you are looking east. Since navigation assigns other directions based on fixed relationships, we know that if you face east, behind you is west. We also know that to your left is north, and to your right is south. In the late afternoon, if you face the sun, you are facing west. Behind you is east. To your right is north, and to your left is south. In the northern hemisphere, near mid-day, your shadow points to the north. In the southern hemisphere, it points south. Knowing this, we can assign the other directions. But how does one know which way is north on a cloudy day?

If you live in an area where moss or lichen grows on trees and rocks, you'll find it mostly growing on the north side of an object. Facing in that direction, you can use the mnemonic Never Eat Soggy Waffles to find the four cardinal directions.

North (never) is in front of you. Moving clockwise (to your right) are the directions east (eat), south (soggy), and west (waffles).

In the northern hemisphere, you can find north at night by locating the Big Dipper constellation. The two stars that form the end of the cup in this constellation point to a star named Polaris, which is also called the North Star. It gets its name from the fact that although all the stars rotate in the sky, the north star remains fixed. Polaris is the first star in the handle of the Little Dipper constellation. When viewed by us, Polaris is always to our north. Once you've found the north star, as you face it, you can use the Never Eat Soggy Waffles mnemonic to find the other cardinal directions. East is to your right, south is behind you, and west is to your left.

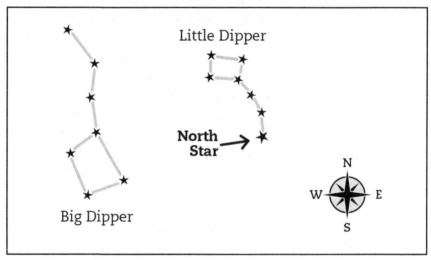

Locating the North Star (Polaris) at night using two constellations

A compass is a device with a magnetic needle that is attracted to the north pole. The needle rotates on a center axis. One end of the compass needle points toward the north. It's typically red and marked with the letter "N." It's important to remember that the magnetic north pole is not found at the geographic north pole. The magnetic north pole is located on Ellesmere Island in northern Canada. There is a slight discrepancy between true north as indicated on a map and magnetic north as indicated by a compass. This discrepancy is called the *magnetic declination,* and it varies based on your location. For general navigation, declination does not need to be considered. For precise navigation, travelers will adjust their direction of travel to account for declination.

Before the advent of cell phones and the internet, people used paper maps and atlases to navigate. **TIP:** It would be wise to procure maps and atlases before a crisis strikes as they may be hard to find afterward. Many towns have a set of streets that run north to south and another set of streets that run east to west. This arrangement is called a street grid. Houses and businesses are assigned numbers that begin at a low number and go higher as one moves north, south, east, or west relative to the starting point. The starting point for numbering is typically a main thoroughfare in the city. There will be one street that runs east to west and one that runs north to south, designated as the points where the numbering system starts. Numbering may begin with a two-digit or a three-digit number. If the first city block has numbers between 100-200, the second block will have numbers between 200-300. The third block will have numbers between 300-400, and so on. Numbers increase block by block on both east-to-west streets and north-south streets. Typically, odd house numbers are assigned on one side of the street, while even numbers are assigned on the other side of the street.

Usually, a direction designator is added to an address, such as N for north, S for south, E for east, and W for west. The letter indicates which direction an address is in relation to the street where the numbering begins.

Let's imagine a town where Main Street is the east-west street where the numbering system begins, and 1st Avenue is the north-south street where the numbering system begins. If I were to start walking north on 1st Avenue from Main Street, houses on the right-hand (east) side of the first block would have addresses such as 125 North 1st Avenue, 157 North 1st Avenue, and 173 North 1st Avenue. Note that as I move away from Main

Street, the numbers grow larger and that all the numbers are odd since they are on the right-hand (east) side of the street. Homes on the opposite side of the street would have numbers such as 122, 156, and 174 North 1st Avenue. Also, note that because I'm traveling north of Main Street, each address has a north designator. If I continued walking, homes in the second block on the east side of the street would have numbers like 219, 237, and 275. Homes on the third block would have numbers like 323, 357 and 379. If I were to walk south on 1st Avenue from Main Street, the house numbers would have a similar configuration except that instead of a north designator, they would have a south designator.

There are other ways in which addresses are assigned. In states like Washington, some cities are divided into geographic quadrants: northeast (NE), northwest (NW), southeast (SE), and southwest (SW). An address is assigned a two-letter designator indicating which quadrant of the city it is in.

Navigating a town with a street grid using a map and compass is a relatively simple process. Most maps have an index that shows where streets can be found by referencing them in relation to vertical columns and horizontal rows on the map. In the above example, Main Street might be found in row G on the map, and 1st Avenue might be located in column 7. If you were at the intersection of Main Street and 1st Avenue, on the map, your position would be found at the intersection of column 7 and row G. For this exercise, let's imagine you wanted to get to 715 North 4th Avenue. The quick way to determine your course would be to note that the 700 block is seven blocks north of Main Street and that 4th Avenue is three blocks east of 1st Avenue. Thus, you would travel three blocks east and seven blocks north to arrive at the approximate location. The number 715 is one of the lower numbers on that block. I would expect the address to be on the corner, on the east side of the street, since it is an odd number.

Navigating from city to city using a map is not difficult, but it does require one to pay close attention to road signs. In most areas, signs along the road near the city limits indicate the name of the city you are entering or leaving.

To navigate to a different city:

- Look up the city you will travel to in a map's index and note the row and column where it is found on the map.

- Find your current location on the map and, using the mileage scale on the map, determine roughly how many miles away the destination is from your present location and make a note of it.

- Note the roads you must take to get to the destination city and the general direction you must travel.

- Use main roads and highways to plot your course if you're not skilled at navigation. If, for example, your present location is three miles north of the highway that leads to your destination city, you will travel three miles south on a road that intersects that highway until you get to the highway. Use a compass if necessary to find the correct direction of travel.

- After driving three miles south, you would then turn left (east) on the highway and travel the required distance to get to the destination city.

- If your destination address is five blocks north of the highway on a street that intersects the highway, turn left (north) when you come to that street. Travel five blocks, and you'll be in the general area. Once there, scan the numbers on the buildings for the street number corresponding to the desired address.

It's a good idea to have a paper map or atlas handy for each city and state where you expect to travel, as well as a compass.

Be advised that all maps are not created equal. Your local chamber of commerce may have a free map of the town, but these maps are designed for tourists and not navigation. Topographic maps are helpful for backcountry exploration, but a standard street map is best for general navigation.

Alternate Transportation

If you use a car or truck as your primary means of transportation, you may have difficulties if it malfunctions or if fuel becomes scarce. Consider acquiring a secondary means of transportation such as a pedal bicycle, electric bike, motorcycle, or electric golf cart.

Spare Fuel

Many types of disasters can lead to fuel shortages. It's wise to store up a supply of fuel for your car, truck, or motorcycle. Keep in mind that gasoline has a short shelf-life, which can be extended by adding a fuel stabilizer to it when it is purchased. Store fuel in an approved container away from heat and sources of ignition.

Auto Emergency Kit

Each vehicle you own should have a spare tire and jack, and an emergency repair kit that includes jumper cables and an assortment of hand tools. If you live in a climate where it snows, have a set of tire chains or a container of cat litter. Cat litter sprinkled under the tires will improve traction on hard packed snow or ice.

Traveling during a crisis can be stressful and dangerous, but when you're adequately preprepared, you'll do it with more confidence and less risk.

7

Financial Risk

UP TO THIS POINT, WE'VE discussed natural and man-made disasters that may cause a crisis. Now, let's consider financial crises that we may want to prepare for. Many situations can expose us to the risk of financial trouble.

> **Disclaimer:** *I am not a licensed financial advisor. I am not qualified to provide advice about personal finances and investing. The information in this chapter is not intended to be a substitute for the advice of a licensed investment advisor. If you feel you need financial advice, please contact a licensed financial advisor.*

To properly assess our exposure to financial risk, we must answer the following questions:

- What potential problems do individuals and society face that involve finances?
- What are the odds that these things will actually happen?
- What would the short-term and long-term consequences be if they did happen?
- How long would it take to recover from them?
- How should we prepare for the most likely events?
- How should we prepare for the most devastating ones?

For most people, there are the risks of job loss, the loss of a working spouse, catastrophic medical expenses, bankruptcy, rising housing prices, and divorce (the average person in the U.S. spends $25,000 to get divorced). We must find out how likely any of them are to happen, how they would affect us, and whether steps can be taken to reduce our exposure to risk.

Some of these risks are a matter of choice. Cities like Los Angeles, San Fransisco, and New York have high costs of living, which are growing more expensive every day. Rather than living where the cost is high, one might choose to live in a rural community, which is likely to be less expensive and safer.

I'm at a low risk of losing my job since I chose to become self-employed. Anyone who wants to avoid the risk of losing their job could find a way to work for themselves, though self-employment creates other risks.

The risk of being hit with catastrophic medical bills can be reduced by having medical insurance. You might also mitigate this risk by maintaining your health by exercising and taking supplements, which decreases the risk of suffering a catastrophic medical event.

If you choose to take steps to maintain a healthy marriage, you can decrease your risk of divorce. My wife and I do this by reading books about marriage and applying the advice provided to keep our marriage strong.

The loss of retirement savings is another risk. The collapse of the housing bubble in 2008 caused a massive stock market sell-off, which wiped out the retirement accounts of many people. While it caught a lot of people off guard, some experts saw the collapse coming and warned about it. Investing is inherently risky, though some investment risks are low while others are high. Most investment advisors suggest having a diversified portfolio of investments, which tends to lower your exposure to risk. When warnings are issued by reputable experts, they should not be dismissed automatically. Discernment should be exercised and you might ask God to give you instruction on how to invest wisely.

In 2010, God gave me dreams directing me to invest in silver, which sold for less than $20 per ounce at the time. We bought silver coins with some of our savings. About a year later, when the price of silver had risen to more than $40 per ounce, we cashed out the silver to make a down-payment on our first home. A few weeks later, the price of silver dropped to $20 an ounce. At a time when many people experienced financial problems, we benefited by following the instruction God gave us.

We can minimize our exposure to financial risk by being aware of events before they happen so we're not caught off guard. If we see a disaster coming, we can take steps to avoid being caught in its wake. Since we can't know the future except by revelation from God, if we want to avoid financial risk, we should seek instruction from God and follow it. If this concept is new to you, I recommend checking out my book *Hearing God's Voice Made Simple.*

The risk of suffering a financially devastating event can be minimized by having some money set aside in savings. A painless way to build up a nest egg is to have money automatically deposited into a savings account each payday.

Although some risk can be avoided by taking certain actions, other risks are beyond our control. If a cyber attack disabled the internet and cellular networks, online banking services would no longer be available. Electronic purchases would be declined. We would not be able to pay bills online or make electronic withdrawals or deposits. The financial world would be thrown into chaos. A loss of the internet for even a week could cause a severe banking crisis.

It's impossible to predict how banks would handle issues like mortgage, auto, and personal loan payments during a prolonged internet outage. One would assume that a debt would still be owed to some entity if one's lending institution failed due to the crisis, but some debts might be written off as a loss. How quickly could banks be expected to make the transition from internet transactions to in-person deposits and withdrawals as was common 50 years ago?

Is it possible to prepare for a banking crisis? Many lessons were learned about this particular risk during the economic collapse of Argentina. Economic collapse typically results from hyperinflation and excessive government debt. When hyperinflation hits, everyday items become extremely expensive. In severe cases, the price of a loaf of bread can double by the hour. Hyperinflation causes government-issued fiat currency to lose value rapidly. When our paper (fiat) money loses its value, gold and silver increase in value relative to it. Although economic collapse is different from a banking crisis caused by an internet disruption, both events share common features.

When people realize they're not able to conduct banking online, they will reflexively go to a local branch and try to make a withdrawal. Banks only keep on hand a small fraction of their depositor's money; the rest they lend out. A sudden increase in bank withdrawals depletes cash supplies, and within days, banks close because they cannot meet the increased demand for withdrawals. During Argentina's economic collapse, many banks that closed in the first week of the crisis never reopened. The closure of banks causes paychecks to be returned for non-sufficient funds. Truck drivers won't drive without being paid. When truck drivers don't show up for work, deliveries grind to a halt and store shelves lay empty. Law enforcement officers, firefighters, and paramedics won't work if they aren't paid. As a banking crisis worsens, public safety employees may not be available to help in an emergency. Life becomes more dangerous by the day.

In situations involving either economic collapse or a banking crisis, items like food, water, and toilet paper quickly become unavailable. People panic and fill up their gas tanks, and fuel stations soon run out of gas. Hoarding impulses take over and a normally polite society turns violent. The greatest risk of being killed or injured during societal chaos is being outside your home during the first 72 hours. If you can avoid leaving your home, you have a much better chance of avoiding injury. Having a pantry stocked with emergency provisions will allow you to remain in your home for long periods of time, putting you at risk less often.

Presently, the U.S. government is $33 trillion in debt (with more than $100 trillion in unfunded liabilities). In 2023, the interest on the federal debt rose to $1 trillion per year, which was more than the total spent on defense. Federal government spending is growing at an unsustainable clip. It's only a matter of time before the U.S. government defaults on its debt. A default by the government on its debt would destroy the banks around the world that are counting on repayment. Such a default would cause a global economic collapse. Economic collapse leads to crises in law enforcement, emergency medicine, and other essential services.

Now, let's look at life during a long-term economic crisis. If retailers are not able to provide food and other goods for several weeks, alternate economies will spring up. When you need items you don't have, consider bartering with neighbors. Meat, eggs, and produce can be traded, as well as dry and canned goods, but so can valuable skills. A ham radio operator can give others news from around the world when the internet is down. This service could be exchanged for something of value. If you have the tools and skills needed to repair damaged homes, you might barter that service for food. Fragile global supply chains are not needed when we do commerce locally. If you need something that isn't available through bartering, you might be able to purchase it at the black and gray markets that predictably appear during an economic collapse. Black markets sell illicit or stolen goods. Gray markets sell items that may or may not come from legitimate sources. If, for example, a food vendor is unable to sell their products to a grocery store, they might sell them to someone who resells to the public at a temporary market set up under a canvas tent in the middle of town.

In his book, *The Modern Survival Manual: Surviving the Economic Collapse,* Fernando Aguirre, who lived through the economic collapse of Argentina, describes how these markets operate and offers tips for buying goods during dangerous times. When banks close and electronic payments are no longer possible, cash becomes king. As long as you have the cash needed to settle a transaction, you can purchase what you need at your local market.

The strategy recommend by Aguirre is to store your wealth in small units—ideally, silver or gold coins. Silver is preferred as it can be used for transactions of smaller value. One ounce silver rounds are less expensive than government minted silver coins. Quarters, dimes, and half dollars minted before 1965 are 90% silver and are regarded as prime currency in an economic crisis. Storing your wealth as precious metal keeps it from being devalued by hyperinflation. As fiat currency loses value, retail prices soar, but so does the value of gold and silver.

When you need to buy provisions, you must find someone you can trust who will exchange your silver coin for an amount of cash. Aguirre cautions people not to do these transactions casually. If you try to sell a large amount of silver or gold, a dishonest trader may think you have a large stash and they might follow you home and rob you. Only deal with people you trust. Bring along a friend who is armed. Only deal in small amounts of gold or silver in a single transaction to avoid becoming a target for theft. Be sure no one follows you home. Once you've made the transaction, the cash can be used to purchase what you need.
TIP: Keep enough cash on hand to conduct all your financial transactions for several months. When electronic payments are not possible, the best option is conducting transactions in cash. That said, it's impractical to store hundreds of thousands (or millions) of dollars in cash. And having a massive store of cash may be a bad investment. In a financial crisis, gold and silver tend to become more valuable compared to cash over time. You might trade $3,000 in cash for an ounce of gold one week, while the same ounce of gold might be sold for $9,000 a month later. If your money was in gold during that time, it appreciated 300 percent. If your money was in cash, it depreciated by the same amount. Have some cash on hand, but if you have excess, it's better to keep it in gold or silver until it is needed. Many

people have precious metal IRAs. Some keep their precious metals in a safe deposit box at a bank. For emergency preparedness, keep both cash and precious metals in a safe in your home or another secure location that only you have access to.

Many people see crypto currencies as a good investment. My concern is how one would conduct transactions without access to the internet, cellular phones or when the power grid is down. I'm sure it can be done, but this book is focused on tested methods that are proven to work during a collapse.

After Economic Collapse

Years ago, God gave me dreams over a span of several weeks where I saw what life would be like after a major economic collapse. I saw a simpler lifestyle reminiscent of how people lived 100 years ago. The pace was slower. There was less stress. Technology was primitive compared to today. In one dream, I saw the creation of a new stock market. One might think that life would be gloomy in a post-collapse world, but it could be better in many ways. I encourage you to look for the positive during times of change. It will give you the motivation you need to keep going.

8

Water

THE HUMAN BODY CAN GO without food for over a month, but will die without water in a few days. In a crisis, whether man-made or natural, water can become scarce. Most preppers place water at the top of their priority list.

If you live in a rural setting, you may have access to a private or community well. Well water is less susceptible to disruption than municipal water distribution systems. Having said that, nearly all water distribution methods rely on electric pumps to move water. During an extended loss of power, water supplies may be temporarily unavailable. Thus, storing a supply of clean drinking water is wise.

While water contained in your home's water heater may be used in a crisis, it can be difficult to access this water, and it will be used up in a few days. Some people routinely fill their bathtubs with water when a storm is approaching. A plastic liner can be purchased to put inside a tub if you don't want water to be contaminated with residue from the tub. Others opt for storing containers of clean water. Fifty-gallon containers can be purchased and filled with water and treated for long-term use. Containers that hold between one and five gallons can be filled at home or purchased pre-filled. Some prefer to stock up on the small plastic bottles of water sold in shrink-wrapped cases at grocery stores.

The first step in preparing for an emergency is setting aside water. As a rule, a supply of clean water equivalent to one gallon a day per person should be stored for whatever duration you anticipate it will be needed. If you're uncertain how long a crisis will last, consider setting aside enough water to last at least one week (7 gallons per person). This is considered the minimum needed for drinking, cooking, and hygiene. Over time, try to build up a larger reserve. Two gallons of water per day per person will provide a safety cushion. This will be your primary supply of drinking water during an emergency. Water stored in a clean plastic or glass container can be chemically disinfected for long-term storage by treating each gallon with five drops of unscented liquid chlorine bleach.

Next, try to find access to a secondary water supply, i.e., a water heater, pool, pond, stream, well, spring, collected rainwater, etc.

Most of us take for granted that our tap water is relatively safe for use. If you live in an area where municipal water treatment facilities are compromised—particularly during a crisis—tap water may be unsafe. Sometimes, hazardous water is self-evident; it may be discolored or have a peculiar odor. Other times, unsafe water has no distinguishing characteristics. It's safest to err on the side of caution and treat questionable water as if it is unsafe.

Water from a chlorinated pool can be purified using one or more of the treatment methods listed below. Water from a saltwater pool cannot, but it can be filtered with a reverse osmosis filter. (Portable reverse osmosis filters cost upwards of $300.) Water from a pond or stream—even if it looks clean and clear—should be filtered and/or chemically treated before it is used. If a neighbor has a pool or pond, in a crisis, consider bartering with them for something of value.

While unsafe water should not be consumed as is, this doesn't mean it is unusable. Unsafe water can be made drinkable through chemical treatment, boiling, and filtration. Regardless of how thirsty you are during a crisis, do not knowingly drink unsafe water if there is a way to purify or filter it, or when a better water source is available.

Microorganisms in water can be killed by bringing it to a full rolling boil for several minutes. The drawback of boiling water is that it requires fuel or electricity that may be in short supply. Chemical purification, either in the form of chlorine bleach or chlorine dioxide tablets, can help remove microorganisms. To treat questionable water with chlorine bleach, add between five and seven drops of bleach to a gallon of water and let it stand for at least 30 minutes before using. To treat water with chlorine dioxide tablets, follow the instructions provided by the manufacturer.

Boiling and chemical treatment do not remove suspended particles or contaminants. If questionable water is treated with chlorine dioxide, bleach, or boiling, it should also be filtered.

Many preppers use large-capacity water filters like the ones made by Berkey. They work well for filtering water for a group of people, but they are not cheap. SurviMate sells a 22-ounce plastic bottle with a built-in four-stage filtration straw that removes bacteria, chemicals, and other impurities. LifeStraw makes a compact filtration device that purifies questionable water. The safest way to use a commercially available filter is to follow the instructions provided by the manufacturer.

If you're starting to prepare for a disaster, storing water should be your highest priority. An inexpensive first purchase would be 7 gallons of water for each person in your family (enough water to last each person one week). You might also consider buying a portable water filtration device for each person in your family. Learn what you can about alternative water sources nearby, and add water to your prepper pantry when you can.

9

Food

IN THE HIERARCHY OF IMPORTANCE for preparedness, right behind water is food. Most people don't think about the possibility of a food shortage, but several types of crises can make food scarce. Most of us buy food that is delivered to a grocery store by a truck that runs on diesel fuel or gasoline. If the price of fuel rises suddenly, or if it becomes unavailable, trucks may not be able to make deliveries. The typical grocery store has enough food inventory to last a few days. During the economic collapse in Argentina, thousands of people died of starvation because fuel was unavailable to keep delivery trucks running. Therefore, it's wise to stock up on food with a long shelf-life.

Food storage is not a one-size-fits-all proposition. Food storage goals can vary from person to person. Each individual should personalize their plan to achieve their particular goals.

Most preppers are not planning for a specific event, and they're not sure when a crisis will hit. They plan for the long term, figuring that a crisis could strike any time over ten or twenty years. If you look at the issue from the long-term perspective, your plan will work best if your food storage solutions provide a shelf life of 10-20 years.

Other preppers have a specific event they're preparing for. Some have identified a window of time during which they expect the event to happen. This prepper doesn't necessarily need to consider a long-term food storage solution in their plan. Shorter-term food storage solutions can be used if the window is two years. This should be kept in mind when considering how you intend to prepare. As a rule, buy things you normally eat, and as you consume them from your pantry, replace them.

If you're new to prepping, a good start is putting together a one-week supply of non-perishable food kept in a dry, secure, temperature-controlled location in your home. Consider starting with canned foods like Spam, chili, soup, tuna, beef, chicken, fruit, and vegetables. Although canned foods have an expiration date, according to the U.S. Department of Agriculture, they have an indefinite shelf-life. As long as the integrity of the can is not compromised, and the food has not spoiled, it can be eaten decades after the expiration date. Once a can has been opened, evaluate the contents for signs of spoilage. After the expiration date, texture and color may change, but the food's nutritional value remains unaffected. Because canned food has an indefinite shelf life, it covers the needs of both short and long-term preppers. If you store canned foods, have a few can openers on hand. Only store what you'll actually eat. The exception is if you intend to store a popular item that will be used for bartering. You might not like Spam, but it's popular with preppers and can be traded for items that are scarce.

The canning process involves heating foods to a high enough temperature to kill bacteria that would cause the food to spoil. As a result, all canned foods are pre-cooked. You may heat them if you want, but it's not necessary. This is an important consideration if access to fuel for cooking is unavailable. Some people can their own foods using glass jars. If this interests you, instructions can be found on many home canning websites.

Other foods to consider are dried beans, rice, oats, pasta, and potatoes. These foods, when dried, have a shelf life of a couple of years, which can be lengthened to 5-10 years by storing them in mylar bags with oxygen absorbers. Many websites and YouTube channels provide information on how to prepare food for long-term storage. Be aware that some foods, like rice and dry beans, require potable water and a lengthy cooking process. Keep this in mind when making your plans.

Dehydrated food has a shelf-life of 4-12 months, depending on the type of food and the storage temperature. The cooler the temperature, the longer food can be stored. Another option for long-term storage is freeze-dried food, which has the moisture removed from it. It is usually reconstituted with water before eating, but it can be consumed without reconstitution.

Years ago, freeze-dried food was a staple of those who ventured into the wilderness, but it's come into vogue recently, and many people preserve their food using commercially made freeze drying machines. Because 98-99 percent of the moisture is removed during the process, freeze-dried food has a shelf life of up to 25 years.

In addition to these foods, consider stocking up on salt, pepper, dried onion, garlic, cayenne, or other favorite spices. You should have on hand some extra flour, oil, and other cooking essentials. If you store dried pasta, consider keeping your favorite sauce to go with it. You may be forced to go through what seems like the end of the world, but you don't have to eat bland food. Honey has an indefinite shelf life and makes a great addition to your prepper pantry.

If your goal for prepping is short-term, consider stocking up on peanut butter, jam, crackers, nuts, instant rice, and other items with a one to two-year shelf life. You should avoid only storing foods that are high in carbohydrates. Be sure to also have foods with high nutritional value, like fruits, vegetables, and meats, which provide needed vitamins and protein. If you're a coffee or tea drinker, consider storing some extra coffee, tea, filters and powdered creamer.

Frozen food can be eaten months after freezing if it has not been thawed and refrozen. Keep in mind that if you rely on frozen food, you'll need a power source to maintain the necessary temperature. If power is lost and you're forced to begin eating your stored food, start with whatever has the shortest shelf-life. Generally, this will include any thing that is frozen or refrigerated. **TIP:** If you live in an area with extremely cold weather, consider storing frozen food outside in a secure container. You might even move your refrigerator outside.

If you have room in your yard, consider planting a garden. You can also grow a garden indoors with the help of grow lights. Consider raising your own livestock. In a crisis, meat and eggs become scarce, but if you raise your own chickens or other animals, you will not be affected as severely, and you'll have things of value for bartering. Growing or raising your own food is an excellent way to remove yourself from dependency on delicate international supply chains, which can easily be disrupted.

Plan for a way to cook the food you store other than an electric stove, i.e., propane stove, gas stove, lightweight backpack stove, solar stove, charcoal grill, etc. Consider putting together a bug-out kit with enough food to sustain you for three days. If you have pets or livestock, consider storing up food for them. In a grid-down crisis, access to water may be limited. Washing dishes could mean using valuable water. Consider stocking up on disposable plates, bowls, cups, forks, knives, and spoons.

A reasonable goal for beginners is putting aside enough food to last one week and then working toward goals of one month, three months, and one year. An inexpensive purchase for someone just beginning would be ten cans of beef, chicken, tuna, soup, or chili.

10

Shelter

YOUR PRIMARY SHELTER IS YOUR home. In a crisis—particularly during times of civil unrest—it becomes a safe haven from the dangers of a society thrown into chaos.

There are several ways to make your home more resilient to the adverse effects of a crisis. If you live in an area prone to earthquakes, consider making structural improvements to your house to increase the odds that it will remain intact during a large quake. If you live in an area prone to tornadoes, you should have a below-ground cellar or basement. If you live in an area prone to flooding, consider keeping a supply of sandbags handy to build a dike that diverts floodwater.

Severe storms or rioting can cause broken windows, which will need to be repaired or boarded up for safety. Plastic sheeting and duct tape can be used to make temporary repairs to broken windows. A tarp can be used to cover a broken window during a storm. Sheets of plywood or oriented strand board (OSB) can be cut to fit the openings of broken windows and doors. Once cut to the needed size, the board is nailed or screwed in place to cover the opening. It's wise to keep on hand a few sheets of plywood (or OSB), tarps, and plastic sheeting. Home repairs can be made if you have a supply of fasteners such as nails and screws, and tools like a battery-powered drill, hammer, tape measure, hand saw, pliers, wrenches, screwdrivers, leather work gloves, pry bar, shovel, axe, wheelbarrow, chain saw, broom, dustpan, and large trash bags.

Home Security

A security system will give you peace of mind during civil unrest. Window and door sensors will let you know if an intruder has entered your home. Here are a few issues to consider if you have a security system: Window and door sensors are usually battery operated. The central receiving unit of most alarm systems is powered by household electric current. Some receiving units have battery backup power. If yours does not, in a power outage, it would need to be plugged it into a generator to work. If your system is monitored by a security company, during an internet outage, they would not be able to provide monitoring service.

A doorbell with a video camera will alert you to the presence of someone at your door. Security cameras that were once expensive are more affordable today, and they'll let you know who is near your property. However, doorbells and cameras that are powered by household current may not operate during a power outage.

Property with no physical barrier to prevent intruders from accessing your home is a risky way to live. Hedges and bushes that are close together may impede an intruder, at least temporarily, but they may also provide cover for burglars. Weigh the potential risks and benefits. A wall that surrounds your property is a good burglar deterrent. Thorny bushes or cacti strategically placed near points of access or beneath windows will make would-be intruders think twice. If your property has an opening in a wall, consider restricting access to it by adding a gate. Wherever you have gates, keep them locked.

One of the weakest security points in a home is the garage door. They are easy to pry open but can be hardened against intrusion by attaching an inexpensive sliding deadbolt device onto the door frame. These locks have a bar that slides through a hole in the door's track. When activated, the garage door cannot be pried open. A step-up in home defense is installing burglar bars or burglar-proof screens over windows and adding security doors to all exterior doorways. The goal is to make your home a difficult target, which will give burglars a preference for an easier home down the street.

The security measures outlined above may help deter a burglar or rioter, but you may find yourself face-to-face with someone who intends to harm you. Remember that you are safest when in your home. Resist the urge to go out of your house and confront rioters or burglars. Don't go outside to engage them, even if they are in your yard. You give up your right to defend your home when you're not in it. Remain inside unless it is absolutely necessary to leave.

Non-lethal means of deterring a potential assailant should always be used first. The exception to the rule is if you believe your life is in imminent danger. Pepper spray, rubber projectiles, and other irritants should be used to deter a potentially violent person, and they should only be used when retreat is not a viable option.

Some jurisdictions have what is called a "castle doctrine." The castle doctrine refers to an exception to the rule to retreat before using deadly force if a party is in their home. In jurisdictions that follow the rule to retreat, a party is first required to retreat before using lethal force so long as it can be done safely. Under the castle doctrine, someone who believes they are being threatened with the immediate use of deadly force can legally respond with a proportional amount of force to deter that threat without first retreating. The castle doctrine is subject to restrictions that differ from jurisdiction to jurisdiction. Not all states and countries follow the castle doctrine. Know the laws in your area regarding the use of lethal measures in defense of your home.

Even if an intruder enters your home, it is wise to warn them and use non-lethal force first as a deterrent. If, however, you believe your life is in danger, you may need to consider the use of lethal force. But do so knowing that you may face criminal charges, even if your local jurisdiction allows the use of lethal force during a home invasion. Understand that drawing a weapon on an assailant may cause them to draw one. The only reason to draw a loaded weapon on someone is if you intend to kill them. If you draw a gun and hesitate, the assailant may kill you.

If you are in a lethal force incident, eventually, law enforcement will respond to investigate. In fact, you can call local law enforcement yourself, but do not try to explain your situation to police or answer questions about what happened. Anything you say—even if you were exercising self-defense—*can* and *will* be used against you in a court of law. This is becoming more true than we'd like to realize. The 5th amendment was written to protect innocent people like you. Unfortunately, even your *true* statements to police may be misquoted in their report. Police may also inaccurately recall your words when they testify in court. The best attorneys will tell you to say nothing. Call a criminal defense attorney for advice or representation in your defense. If you are a gun owner, it's wise to research attorneys ahead of time and be prepared for situations like this. There are 2nd amendment groups that help gun owners with legal representation, but most require that you join the group prior to any gun incident.

Fernando Aguirre tells of how, during Argentina's economic collapse, gangs of marauders waited nearby for people to come out of their homes to ambush them. Aguirre developed a habit of having someone look out the window to see if anyone was waiting outside before he would leave his home. A similar situation would happen when he returned. Frequently, he'd find robbers waiting near his home, hoping to rush and overpower him as he went inside. He would yell out a warning for them to leave, then drive around the block. He would show them his gun if they were still there when he returned, which usually convinced them to leave.

At some point, you may be confronted by forces that overwhelm your ability to remain safe in your home. This is when you should consider leaving it for another location. It's best to plan a location before an actual emergency, if possible.

Bugging Out

You can control the environment of your home, but when you leave it and go out into the world, you lose that control. As a general rule, during a crisis, you should remain in your home as long as it's safe to do so. Resist the urge to leave (bug-out), as once you do, your now-vacant home may become a home for looters, and you may not be able to return to it.

If you decide to leave, the best option is to go to another controlled environment where you are safe. A second home is an ideal bug-out location because you will be in control of the property. If you have a second home, be sure it is stocked with essential items needed for survival. When staying at your primary residence becomes untenable, take whatever items you need and leave, taking the safest route to the bug-out location, even if that route is not the most convenient. Having a paper map with your primary and secondary routes to this location highlighted may be helpful. When you arrive, scan the local area to see if it is safe. If your second home is also under imminent threat, consider other options.

Factor into your plan the option to live temporarily with a relative or friend you trust. You might agree mutually to shelter one another if one person's home becomes unlivable. When it is time to leave, notify them, gather necessities, and take the safest route to their location.

Another option is using a recreational vehicle as a bug-out shelter. RVs are less resistant to break-ins, but they're mobile, and you may be able to drive to a safe location. Most RVs have the essentials needed to survive temporarily—a supply of water, cooking facilities, a bed, and a bathroom.

Your car or truck can be used as a temporary shelter. If this option becomes necessary, find a safe place to park, ideally near a location that offers food, water, and a bathroom. Keep your vehicle doors locked at all times.

A less desirable but workable alternative is a tent with a sleeping bag, cook stove, food, water, and whatever supplies you can bring with you from your home. A tent is a short-term solution. Every day you're in a tent, you should look for a better long-term solution. A tent is not a safe shelter when thieves are looking for an easy mark, but it's a reasonable option while seeking a better alternative. If you choose to camp at a public campground, assess the local scene and try to determine if troublemakers are nearby. If a campground is unsafe, consider finding a secluded location off the beaten path. The risk of camping in such a location is that you're highly vulnerable to attack if someone happens to find you.

Essential Items for Survival

The items needed for survival away from home vary depending on the type of crisis and one's activities. For starters, I recommend setting aside several bottles of water and a supply of non-perishable foods. Here are a few other items to consider:

Fire Starter: One of the primary needs for off-grid survival is a fire. It provides light, heat, and an emotional boost when you're discouraged. If you've ever tried to start a fire with wet matches, you'll understand why it's important to carry at least one device that can quickly start a fire in any weather. A butane lighter is one option, but it may not work well in cold temperatures due to the low vapor pressure of butane when the ambient temperature is below freezing. If you warm a butane lighter, it may work, but it's wise to have another option. Consider carrying a ferro rod. A ferro rod is a cylindrical tool made of a metal alloy that produces sparks when scraped against a hard surface, like the back of a knife blade. Pair this with a bag of magnesium shavings, and you have a bombproof way to start a fire even during a downpour. For any item that is critical to survival, you may want to consider having a spare in case the primary one becomes lost or broken.

Portable Stove: If you will need to cook, consider purchasing a compact camping stove that burns hexamine blocks.

Water Container: Whether metal or plastic, it's imperative to have a container to carry and decontaminate water.

Knife or Multi-tool: In a crisis, a knife can be used for food preparation, cutting tinder and wood, starting fires, first aid, self-defense, and campsite preparation.

Portable Light: Whether a handheld flashlight, headlamp, or some other device, be sure to carry at least one portable source of illumination.

Cordage: A field expedient shelter can be erected with a length of paracord and a tarp. Nylon paracord has many other practical uses and is sold in different sizes. I like 550 paracord, which is four millimeters in diameter. (It gets it's name from the fact that it has a breaking strength of 550 lbs.) A less expensive alternative is three millimeter paracord. It has a breaking strength of 325 pounds and is good for applications where lighter weight cord is preferable.

Blanket or Tarp: Whether a thin mylar space blanket or a plastic tarp, consider carrying a piece of material that can keep you dry in the rain and warm when it's cold. A tarp can be used as a makeshift sleeping shelter, and one that is the same color as the local foliage can provide concealment from an enemy.

Tent and Sleeping Bag: A sleeping bag and tent will keep you warm and dry at night when away from home. The weight of the sleeping bag should take into consideration your local climate. The size of the tent should be determined by how many people you expect to need shelter.

Compass and Map: Carry a compass on you at all times during a crisis. Ideally, you'll want one with a mirror, which, in addition to helping with navigation, can be used for personal hygiene and signaling for help. Consider securing the compass to your clothing to avoid losing it. Have on hand a physical map of the local area.

Bandana: A square piece of 100% cotton cloth can be used for filtering large particles from water of questionable quality. It can also be used as a bandage, a tourniquet, as tinder for starting a fire, and even for signaling a rescue team if it happens to be a bright color.

First Aid Kit: Carry a plastic sandwich bag stocked with gauze dressings, roller bandages, antibiotic ointment, and Band-Aids.

Duct Tape: Emergencies often call for improvised solutions. Duct tape can be used for making repairs, and it makes a good emergency bandage.

Backpack: The easiest way to carry or store the items you'll need is in a quality backpack. Be sure to pick one that fits the items on your list and is comfortable to wear for long periods of time.

Body Armor: If you're forced to live or travel in an uncontrolled environment, wearing body armor will give you a better chance of survival.

Living away from home is not a permanent situation. When the crisis abates, you will return to a more stable lifestyle, though it may be different from the one you were accustomed to living. Adapt. Improvise. Make the needed adjustments. Determine in your heart that you will not be defeated. The human mind, when properly conditioned, can overcome any adversity.

11

Firearms

MANY CHRISTIANS BELIEVE THAT THE Bible prohibits the use of weapons for self-defense. The proof text usually provided is the account where Peter cut off the ear of the High Priest's servant with a sword and was rebuked by Jesus. Here is that story from the gospel of Matthew:

> The traitor, Judas, had given them a prearranged signal: "You will know which one to arrest when I greet him with a kiss." So Judas came straight to Jesus. "Greetings, Rabbi!" he exclaimed and gave him the kiss.
> Jesus said, "My friend, go ahead and do what you have come for."
> Then the others grabbed Jesus and arrested him. But one of the men with Jesus pulled out his sword and struck the high Priest's slave, slashing off his ear.
> "Put away your sword," Jesus told him. "Those who use the sword will die by the sword. Don't you realize that I could ask my Father for thousands of angels to protect us, and he would send them instantly? But if I did, how would the Scriptures be fulfilled that describe what must happen now?"
> MATT. 26:48-54 NLT

In his gospel, the Apostle John identified the disciple as Peter. The context was that Jesus had told His disciples He would be crucified. They did not accept His warning. They understood that the Messiah would rule as King of Israel and destroy the kingdom of Rome. When Jesus was about to be taken away and crucified, Peter drew his sword and struck the high Priest's servant, thinking it was time for an offensive operation. Jesus then explained two separate principles. He reminded them that He must be crucified because it was the very reason why He came to Earth. He, a perfectly innocent man, would be made a sacrifice to atone for the sins of the world. Peter's attempt to defend Him was in opposition to God's plan.

As an aside, the Lord reminded Peter that those who live by the sword shall die by the sword. What does this mean exactly?

Some take this admonishment to be a prohibition against any violence—and in particular—against armed self-defense.

In context, Jesus referred to someone who uses deadly force to get what they want. Peter wanted to prevent the death of his master and thought violence would help. Burglars, murderers, and terrorists use force to attain their goals. Police officers and law-abiding citizens use force to counteract lawlessness. Force isn't always used for evil. It may have either malevolent or benevolent goals.

Some say that Jesus prohibited His disciples from carrying weapons for self-defense. We know that He did not make such a prohibition. Before Peter attacked the High Priest's servant, Jesus told the disciples to arm themselves. Here's the account from the gospel of Luke:

Then Jesus asked them, "When I sent you out to preach the Good News and you did not have money, a traveler's bag, or an extra pair of sandals, did you need anything?"

"No," they replied.

"But now," he said, "take your money and a traveler's bag. And if you don't have a sword, sell your cloak and buy one! For the time has come for this prophecy about me to be fulfilled: 'He was counted among the rebels.' Yes, everything written about me by the prophets will come true."

LUKE 22:35-37 NLT

Previously, the Lord sent them out without weapons, but now that He was about to die, He told them to take up arms. Ten verses later, they told Him they did as He instructed and brought swords:

> But even as Jesus said this, a crowd approached, led by Judas, one of the twelve disciples. Judas walked over to Jesus to greet him with a kiss. But Jesus said, "Judas, would you betray the Son of Man with a kiss?"
>
> When the other disciples saw what was about to happen, they exclaimed, "Lord, should we fight? We brought the swords!" And one of them struck at the high Priest's slave, slashing off his right ear.
>
> LUKE 22:47-50 NLT

Jesus explicitly told His disciples to arm themselves with deadly weapons. The incident with Peter gave Him an opportunity to teach them *when* the use of force was appropriate. That being the case, the rest of this chapter will provide suggestions for the wise use of deadly force in self-defense.

In locations where firearm ownership is permitted, many people find it beneficial to own a gun for personal and home defense. If you own a gun, a supply of ammunition is needed, which becomes an issue when considering preparedness. In times of societal unrest, some calibers of ammunition will not be available. Choosing a gun chambered for ammunition that is available in a worst-case scenario is a wise decision. The best all-around survival ammunition is 22LR. It's cheap, versatile, and widely available. For pistols, 9-millimeter is the most widely used and widely available round in the world. For rifles, 308 and 223 Remington are the most widely available rounds.

Guns are machines. They're tools that can accomplish certain things, like any other tool. No one tool is perfect for all the jobs that tools must do. A hammer is great if the job requires driving a nail into a board. But it's lousy if you need to drill a hole. Like other tools, different types of guns are designed to do different types of work, and no single firearm will do everything that you might need the weapon to do.

In a prolonged crisis, access to ammunition, spare parts, and knowing someone who can repair your firearm are potential problems. Durability, reliability, and a weapon that does not require a degree in mechanical engineering to take apart and clean is a high priority for me. Some guns are easier to disassemble, clean, and repair, while some are less prone to mechanical failure than others. Owning a popular firearm increases the chance that spare parts will be available in a crisis and that someone you know will be able to repair it.

In recent years, many types of ammunition were stockpiled by citizens and became unavailable in retail stores for months due to increased public concern over gun legislation. History demonstrates that when people get nervous, they stockpile ammunition, leaving retail inventories low. If ammunition for your weapon is hard to find when a few gun laws are passed, imagine how scarce it will be during a major crisis. For that reason, owning guns that have readily available ammunition is imperative.

Below is a list of guns you might consider owning. My recommendations take into consideration durability, reliability, ease of repair, and the likelihood that ammunition will be available during a crisis. If you're like most people, you have a limited budget. So, you'll have to choose which guns you should purchase first and which must wait. With that in mind, here are some guns to consider owning:

22 Rifle or Pistol

The 22 caliber long rifle (22LR) is the most commonly sold round in the world and is likely to be the most available in a crisis. It's also one of the lightest and least expensive rounds to carry. The fact that the 22 caliber round can be used in both rifles and pistols also makes it highly versatile. A 22 rifle can take down most small game, making it a good choice for hunting. If you're new to handguns, starting with a 22 pistol is a good choice. It has little recoil, is light, easy to carry, and easy to shoot.

Full-Size Pistol

The pistol is the gun you're most likely to have access to at home or in public. Owning a full-sized pistol is critical to proper self and home defense. By "full-size" pistol, I mean one with a barrel length of three to five inches. Semi-automatic models are preferred due to larger capacity magazines than the standard five or six rounds of a revolver. The minimum magazine capacity should be 13 rounds; 17 rounds or more is ideal. If you live in California, you'll be limited in magazine capacity. Check your local laws to learn what you can legally own in your state or country.

Most experts agree that the minimum caliber for effectively stopping an attacker is 9 millimeter. Some people prefer the larger 40 and 45 caliber rounds, but they're more expensive, and the stopping power is not much better than the 9 millimeter.

My handgun of choice is a model that has little recoil compared to its competitors, holds plenty of rounds, and I can shoot it accurately. I can't recommend a particular pistol for you because what works well for me may not work for you. If you want to buy a pistol but don't know which model is best, do what I did. Go to a shooting range that rents guns. Fire every full-size pistol they have. If you find one that feels good and you can fire it accurately, buy it. The most expensive gun in the world is useless if you can't hit what you're shooting at. I recommend taking a handgun safety course if you've never owned a gun. When I took my first firearms safety course, it included supervised range time to test a variety of available handguns.

When purchasing a gun, consider one with a record for reliability. Pistols that are known to have problems with failure to feed and failure to fire should be avoided. Sometimes, this is caused by a problem with the pistol. More often, it's a problem with the ammunition.

Not all ammunition is made equal. High-quality ammunition is less prone to problems with failing to fire or feed. Less expensive rounds may feed and fire reliably, or they may not. If you find a manufacturer that produces a quality round at a reasonable price, stock up, and you won't have to worry about this issue.

Here's a suggestion regarding the choice of ammunition: The two most common types of rounds are full metal jacket (FMJ) and hollow point (HP or JHP). Hollow point rounds are preferred for self-defense for a couple of reasons. A hollow point round mushrooms on impact, which reduces its velocity. The energy of the round is absorbed by the target, meaning the hollow point has greater stopping power when compared to a full metal jacket round that does not mushroom. But there's another reason why they are preferred for self-defense. If you fire a hollow point round at an intruder and it misses them, if the bullet passes through the exterior wall of your home, it's likely to fall harmlessly in the yard due to its decreased velocity. Whereas, a full metal jacket round may travel across the street and strike an innocent bystander. Many people use full metal jacket rounds at the shooting range and hollow points for home and self-defense.

Avoid pistols that use odd caliber ammunition such as 10 millimeter and 357 Sig. These rounds will be hard to find in a crisis. The safest bets are models used by the military and police. Manufacturers like Glock, Ruger, Springfield, Smith & Wesson, Sig Sauer, and Beretta sell guns chambered in 9 millimeter, 40 and 45 calibers. Military and law enforcement professionals choose these guns because of their reliability. Ammunition for them can be purchased in bulk, and they should be available (albeit at a much higher price) in a crisis.

Compact Semi-Automatic

When not at home, many people carry a small semi-automatic pistol in a concealed manner. Typically, these weapons weigh less than a pound, can be worn inside the waistband, and have a magazine capacity of six or seven rounds. Most models fire 380 or 9 millimeter rounds. In addition to being small, they're usually less expensive than a full-sized pistol. Some jurisdictions allow the concealed carry of firearms, while others do not. Check your local statutes to be sure you're in compliance.

357 Revolver

The 357 Magnum revolver should be considered if you have trouble operating the slide of a semi-automatic pistol. This weapon was a favorite of law enforcement officers for decades due to its reliability and ease of use. It fires 357 magnum rounds but can also use 38 special, which are inexpensive and similar in stopping power to the 9 millimeter.

AR-15

The AR-15 is the most popular rifle in the world. It has a record for durability (though perhaps not on par with the AK-47). It's a reliable weapon, and some models are inexpensive to buy. It fires 223 Remington and 556 NATO rounds, which are cost effective and should be available, even in a crisis. Because of its popularity, spare parts should be available when needed, and there's a good chance someone you know will be able to help repair it. Spare magazines are cheap, so be sure to have extras on hand. The AR-15 can be outfitted with various accessories, but I don't advise adding a lot of gear to your rifle. Each item added will make it heavier and more difficult to fire accurately. An optic is a logical addition. A tactical light is helpful for positively identifying potential targets in the dark. Look for optics and lights that have positive online reviews, good durability, and ones that use common battery types.

12 Gauge Shotgun

The 12 gauge shotgun should be considered as it can fill multiple roles. Its ability to fire birdshot, buckshot, and slugs makes it a versatile tool that can be used for everything from hunting large game to varmint control and home defense.

Summary

Owning a gun will do you little good in a crisis if you're not competent when operating it and confident you can hit a target. Firearm skills diminish over time. Taking your guns to a range and firing them regularly is important. With some guns, you can perform dry fire practice at home using snap caps, which are simulated rounds that don't harm firing pins.

For all guns, consider stocking up on ammunition when it's cheap. Purchase additional magazines or speed loaders and keep a few of them loaded at all times. Rotate magazines each month to avoid excessive wear on the springs. Consider getting a good holster and a couple of magazine pouches (or speed loader pouches for revolvers).

12

Where to Live

PREVIOUSLY, WE LOOKED AT THE risk natural disasters pose to people who live in certain geographic locations. Next, let's examine the risks and benefits of living in an urban environment versus living in a rural or suburban setting during a man-made crisis.

The Urban Jungle

If you live in an urban environment, a variety of issues should be factored into your plans. Large cities are the most likely targets for terrorism. When someone wants to make a statement by hurting or killing a large number of people, they tend to target major metropolitan areas. You're much more likely to be exposed to a nuclear bomb detonation in New York, than in Iowa. You should weigh the risk of terrorism when deciding where to live before and during an extended crisis. Certain industrial complexes and military installations are at a higher risk of being targeted by an enemy during war. That risk should also be considered.

Times of crisis can make it hard just to find a meal and a safe place to sleep. There is usually more access to help from government and non-government agencies in urban areas during a crisis. Shelters that provide a place to sleep and a meal are more common in large cities. If you have not prepared, or if you find yourself on the road during a crisis, this ought to be considered. There is usually better access to public transportation (if it's available) in urban areas. If you must travel, factor this into your plans.

The availability of law-enforcement is generally better in urban areas than in rural ones. But during a crisis, it is not uncommon for law-enforcement to be overwhelmed with calls for help. Their attention is usually drawn to the most severe problems like areas where rioting is taking place. Personal assaults and robberies are given low priority. In a severe or prolonged crisis, you may not be able to count on help from law-enforcement regardless of where you live.

The downsides to living in an urban area during a crisis are numerous. A higher population means more targets for thieves and gangs that take what they want from defenseless people. Many criminals are drawn to urban areas during a crisis. There are more opportunities for you to be assaulted, raped, or robbed in the city. When public services stop, garbage piles up quickly and sewer services may be cut off. In a severe or prolonged crisis, piles of dead bodies can be found strewn through the streets of large cities. These conditions create a perfect environment for the outbreak of disease. Urban areas can quickly become a breeding ground for bacterial infections carried by rats, mosquitoes, and other vectors of transmission.

In times of severe crisis, you should carefully weigh the pros and cons of traveling and living in large cities. The risks will often outweigh the benefits.

Rural Risks

A serene piece of land in the country is the preferred location of many preppers. The availability of acreage for gardening and raising animals and having some distance between your safe house and a major city makes a rural piece of land a good choice. But there are dangers to be considered.

The main drawback of a rural location is isolation from others. For the same reason that some people would choose a remote location, others would choose somewhere else. An isolated location makes you vulnerable to marauding gangs. Although gang activity is more common in urban areas, a few gangs find the isolated, rural location a prime target. They seek out people who live alone, away from friends and neighbors. With a group of armed thugs, the game is to overpower the lone inhabitant or family. If you're willing to take your chances with a rural location, do so knowing that it has this drawback.

If you live in an isolated location, take measures to secure the perimeter of the property against invasion. Consider networking with others in your area to form a team. You might share the responsibility of helping one another when trouble comes and designate one location as a rally point where the group can meet to defend themselves collectively.

Safety in Numbers

Fernando Aguirre wrote that the communities that fared best during Argentina's collapse were those where people came together, pooled their resources, and protected one another. These mostly suburban neighborhoods seldom saw gang related violence and they tended to prosper. If you can recruit a team of people to help defend your castle, you have a better chance of keeping your home intact. If you're not particularly attached to your residence, you might offer to join a group using another property as their base of operations. There is strength in numbers. **TIP:** If you're not acquainted with your neighbors, you might consider getting to know them before you need them for help. A community with strong ties between its members is generally a safe place to live.

13

Hygiene and Sanitation

MODERN SOCIETIES OFFER LONGER LIFESPANS to their citizens largely by mitigating sickness and death through better sanitation. In a widespread disaster, sanitation is one of the first things to falter. During the economic collapse in Argentina, because municipal sanitation workers were not paid, they did not come to work. Garbage quickly piled up, which became a vector for disease. Many people died of illnesses that were non-existent in their cities just a few years earlier. If one wants to survive and thrive during times of chaos, one must put into practice a sensible hygiene and sanitation protocol.

Many people are accustomed to having their trash picked up and taken to a landfill. As mentioned, in times of crisis, this service may not be available. You may have to collect your own trash and take it to a landfill. Do you have a vehicle that can be used to do this? Would you be able to find the nearest landfill if your favorite navigation app was not available? It would be wise to give this some consideration now, before a crisis hits. **TIP:** Locate your nearest landfill and write down the directions to it from your home. Print out the directions and keep them in a safe place.

If your water supply was suddenly disrupted, have you thought about how your daily hygiene would be affected? The usual way to flush a toilet uses water from the toilet tank. If your home's water supply has been disrupted, there is another way. Water from any source can be carried in a bucket and poured into the toilet bowl. One or two gallons is adequate. Pour the water into the toilet bowl slowly at first and then dump the remaining water in quickly. The bowl should empty due to the increased water pressure. An alternative is to dump a gallon or two of water from the bucket into the tank after removing the lid and flushing it as you would normally.

In addition to water not being available, municipal sewers and septic systems may not be operational in a crisis. Have you thought about how to remove human waste from your home in an emergency if flushing the toilet isn't an option? One option is to place a plastic trash bag (tape may be needed to keep the bag in place) beneath a toilet seat to collect waste, which can be stored in a container outside the home and taken to the landfill, or the contents can be buried. A second option is to dig a hole away from your home which is used as a toilet. Bury the waste immediately. A variation on this is to dig a shallow a trench with the earth mounded behind it. Begin by using one end of the trench as an earthen toilet. Move from one end to the other as needed, burying the waste each time the trench is used.

Sacrifices must be made when water is scarce. Daily showers are not a wise use of resources. During a crisis, showering may need to be reduced to once or twice a week, and shorter showers will conserve water. If municipal or well water is not available to take a regular shower, there's another way to do it. A solar shower is a 2-3 gallon bag filled with water and left in the sun, which heats it. Once the water has been warmed, the bag is hoisted to a suitable elevation. A solar shower can be used inside if a support is available to suspend it overhead or it can be secured outside to a tree branch or pergola using paracord. The bag has a hose with a nozzle that is opened to release the water, which lasts a few minutes—long enough for a quick shower. For privacy, a plastic tarp can be suspended from a tree branch with a bungee cord or paracord. (Tarps, paracord, and bungee cords have many uses in an emergency. Keep a supply of them handy.)

Hand washing can prevent the spread of disease, but it can also waste valuable water. Many people routinely use liquid hand sanitizer. A discussion of when to use soap and when to use hand sanitizer is in order. Soap contains surfactants, which remove dirt and contaminants from the skin. All hand soaps are antibacterial. Hand sanitizer contains alcohol, which kills bacteria and viruses, but does not remove dirt and other contaminants. If the concern is avoiding the spread of bacterial or viral pathogens, hand sanitizer can be used. But if the problem is contamination from some other substance, washing with soap is a better option. Use as little water as possible. In addition to hand soap and sanitizer, consider stocking up on disposable prepackaged hand or baby wipes.

Many people found out during the covid pandemic of 2020 just how sensitive the toilet paper supply chain is. It's a good idea to stock up on toilet paper, tissues, paper towels, tampons, and other paper products before a crisis. If you're just beginning your prepping journey, consider gradually building up an inventory of soap, shampoo, conditioner, toothpaste, dental floss, Q-tips, razor blades, shaving cream, toilet paper, tissues, and other personal hygiene items. Avoid waiting until everyone is shopping for these items. When the crisis occurs, if you're in a position to share, you can help family or neighbors in need of supplies.

14

Emergency First Aid

THE TREATMENT OF ILLNESS AND injury should be a part of every preparedness plan. Even minor disasters can overwhelm hospitals and emergency medical services (EMS), making it impossible to provide aid to everyone who needs it. In a major disaster, medical supplies and staff are quickly exhausted. A severe crisis can leave a community without medical treatment for weeks or months. The advice provided herein is given under the assumption that treatment by a licensed medical professional will be delayed or is unavailable. Treatment by a trained medical team is always preferable except for cases where the illness or injury is mild. If you're not able to arrange transport of the seriously sick or injured person to a hospital, you must do the best you can with whatever personnel and resources you have. In this chapter, I'll provide some basic information about treating common illnesses and injuries.

The Assessment

Providing the right treatment for an illness or injury requires an accurate assessment. Although some medical conditions can be assessed visually, important information can be obtained by getting a set of vital signs. Basic vital signs include the respiratory rate, heart rate, blood pressure, oxygen saturation, and mental status.

The respiratory rate is the number of breaths taken per minute. It can be calculated by observing someone's breathing and counting their breaths over 30 seconds and multiplying the number by two. Normal, healthy adults breathe between 10 and 20 times per minute. A secondary consideration is the work of breathing. How much exertion is required for the person to take a breath? Is their breathing labored, or does their work of breathing seem normal?

The heart rate is usually calculated by feeling the person's pulse by placing two fingers along the wrist just below the thumb. The pulse rate is determined by counting the number of beats felt in 30 seconds and multiplying it by two. The heart rate of a normal, healthy adult should be between 60-100.

If you have a way to measure blood pressure, it will be helpful. The textbook normal blood pressure is 120/80. The higher (systolic) number may be considered normal if it is between 100-140. The lower (diastolic) number may be considered normal if it is between 60-90. At the time of this writing, automatic blood pressure monitors can be purchased for as little as $12.

A pulse oximeter measures the amount of oxygen in the blood. Most pulse oximetry devices show both the heart rate and oxygen level. The normal oxygen level is above 95. People with chronic respiratory diseases such as COPD or asthma may have lower normal values. Carbon monoxide displaces oxygen in the blood. Because it contains oxygen molecules, a person with carbon monoxide poisoning may have a false normal pulse oximetry reading. Currently, pulse oximetry units can be purchased for around $10.

Mental status is evaluated by assessing the person's alertness. The mnemonic AVPU can be used, which asks what type of stimulus is required to get a response from the individual. Are they alert? (A) Do they respond only to verbal stimulus? (V) Do they respond only to pain? (P) Are they completely unresponsive? (U)

What is considered normal with respect to vital signs is not an exact science. Normal vital signs for one person may be abnormal for someone else. Knowing someone's normal vital signs is another important piece of information. The vital signs you obtain should always be compared to the person's normal vital signs. Vital signs should be considered a snapshot in time. They inform us of a person's condition when they're taken, but they change as the person's condition worsens or improves. It's important to reassess vital signs periodically to detect any changes. The more information you have, the better your chances will be of making an informed treatment decision.

ABCs

Medical personnel are trained to assess airway, breathing, and circulation first. (The mnemonic ABC is used to remind us of the order in which these are assessed. A is for Airway, B is for Breathing, C is for Circulation.) Problems in these areas tend to be fatal if not corrected. We want to know if the person is breathing, how reliable is their airway, do they have a pulse, and do they have any life-threatening bleeding?

If a person has an obstructed airway that is preventing them from breathing adequately, you can assist them by changing the position of their head. When the neck is flexed (when the chin is pointed downward toward the chest), breathing can be compromised. Sometimes, lifting the chin can restore normal breathing. If the person is not breathing (or not breathing adequately), you can assist their respirations, initially with a pocket or bag-valve mask if you have one. If you don't have a mask handy, you must decide if you're willing to give them mouth to mouth ventilation.

Next, you will need to check for a pulse by pressing a couple of fingers in the natural groove in the neck that lies between the windpipe (trachea) and the hard muscle on the side of the neck (sternocleidomastoid). If you feel their heartbeat, they have a pulse. If you do not feel a pulse, the next step is to start cardiac compressions. (If you're interested in learning first aid and CPR, contact your local chapter of the Red Cross or the American Heart Association.)

Medical treatment during a crisis is different from the treatment you would normally give. In a normal situation, when faced with a person who is not breathing and has no pulse, the best treatment is to call for EMS and start CPR. You perform CPR to circulate blood until paramedics arrive with a defibrillator. If they arrive quickly, there's a small chance they may be able to restore circulation by shocking the heart. However, the odds for a successful resuscitation are never good. About 5% of the time, a pulse is restored. Afterward, the individual spends several days or weeks in an ICU, and most of the time, they never regain consciousness.

If EMS is available in such an emergency, they should be contacted. But if they're not available, who is going to get the person to a hospital? What are their chances for survival? It's a reasonable decision to opt not to perform CPR. And in fact, medical triage guidelines recommend that this is the correct decision when a you don't have access to adequate treatment facilities or personnel. The principles of triage dictate that we should help those who have a reasonable chance of surviving when the care we have to offer them is provided. When resources are limited, difficult choices must be made. That may mean not treating someone in cardiac arrest. Next, we'll look at common medical problems and their treatment.

Stings from Plants and Insects

With only a few exceptions, venomous stings from both plants and insects can be treated with one simple remedy. I discovered it years ago, and I've used it with good results on everything from bee stings, to bites from fire ants and brushes with stinging nettle. Most stinging plants and insects use the same chemical in their venom. That chemical is formic acid. Although each insect or plant has a slight twist on the other compounds they produce, the active ingredient is usually formic acid. The antidote is any good alkaline substance that can neutralize this acid. I use baking soda. The treatment is to mix a small amount of water into a few tablespoons of baking soda to make a thick paste. Do not add more water than is necessary to just wet it thoroughly. Apply the paste to the affected area and let it sit on the skin for a few minutes to dry. After it dries, you can resume your normal activities and the paste will eventually fall off.

When I first encountered bites from fire ants here in Arizona, the bites itched and stung for several days afterward and they left large red welts on my skin. After using this remedy, the pain and itching subsided immediately and soon there was no sign that I'd even been bitten.

Snakes, Spiders, and Scorpions

Venomous snake and spider bites are treated by applying a clean dressing to the wound if there is bleeding. If symptoms such as nausea, vomiting, diarrhea, labored breathing, rapid heart rate, blurred vision, increased sweating, or muscle twitching develop, seek treatment at a medical facility.

Scorpion venom is a neurotoxin. In adults, the area that is stung is initially painful, but later, the venom can affect the nervous system, and numbness may develop in the affected body part that can last several weeks. Small children can become seriously ill from scorpion stings and may need to be hospitalized and receive anti-venom.

Burns

Your own safety should be considered before giving aid to someone who has been burned. If they sustained a thermal burn, be sure to identify the source of the injury and make sure it cannot harm you. If the source is electrical, make sure the device that caused the burn is unplugged. For chemical burns, be sure to wear gloves before touching the affected person to avoid becoming contaminated.

Minor burns do not generally require special treatment, though they can be painful. To care for a minor burn with intact skin, it's safe to apply ice for a few minutes to stop the burning process. Apply a dry dressing and antibiotic ointment if there is an open wound. As a general rule, blisters should be left intact to preserve skin integrity. Once a blister is popped, the chance of infection increases and it must be cared for like any other open wound. The exception to the above treatment is a chemical burn. For a chemical burn, the chemical should be brushed off the skin using a gloved hand and the affected area should be rinsed with water for several minutes. A clean, dry dressing can then be applied. More severe burns will require hospital treatment, particularly if the integrity of the skin is compromised. An open wound can become infected and infection can lead to sepsis, which can be life threatening. Burns to the face are dangerous, especially if the airway is involved. If someone sustains burns to their airway, they may display signs of respiratory distress. If wheezing or labored breathing are present, they should be transported to a hospital for evaluation and treatment.

Broken Bones

Broken bones that require treatment before the individual is transported to a hospital are rare. It's difficult to diagnose a broken bone without an x-ray (unless it's an angulated fracture). If a broken bone is suspected, the goal is to immobilize the injured part of the body to the best of your ability and control any bleeding. Immobilization of the leg or arm can be done using a commercially available aluminum splint. Alternatively, a stick approximately two feet long can be used. The splint is placed alongside the injured limb and secured with roller bandages, paracord or cloth strips. A makeshift splint can made from a rectangular piece of cardboard scored on one side and folded, then taped in place around the injured extremity.

Strains and Sprains

Muscles and ligaments that are strained or sprained are best treated using the mnemonic ICE, which stands for ice, compression, and elevation. For the first 48 hours, apply ice to the injury. To avoid damaging the skin, make sure a layer of cloth is placed between the ice and skin. Pre-made cold packs work well. Snow contained inside a plastic bag will work in a pinch.

An Ace elastic bandage can be applied to compress the soft tissue and reduce swelling. If the injury is to the ankle, knee, or elbow, it can be elevated, which will also help reduce swelling.

If immobilization of a joint is needed, a pillow shaped to conform to the joint can be taped around it as a splint. If the injury is to the arm, a triangular bandage can be used to immobilize it. (A triangular bandage is a precut piece of cloth. It is a standard item found in many first aid kits. It can also be purchased at a pharmacy or online.)

Here's how to immobilize an injured arm. The arm is positioned with the elbow flexed, so the lower arm is at 90 degrees to the upper arm. The widest part of the triangular bandage is positioned to support the lower arm with one end of the bandage brought up to the right side of the neck while the other end is brought up to the left side of the neck. The ends of the bandage are tied in a knot behind (or to the side of) the neck. If more immobilization is needed, a second triangular bandage can be tied around the torso and upper arm.

Dehydration

It is commonly understood that dehydration is equivalent to a loss of body fluid. While this understanding is not incorrect, it's not the whole story. In addition to fluids, the body loses electrolytes. Signs of dehydration are confusion, weakness, dizziness, syncope (unconsciousness), fast heart rate, and low blood pressure. Treatment of dehydration is rehydration. If the person can drink, they can be given fluids with electrolytes. Sports drinks or coconut water can be used. Pedialyte is another option. Because I live in the desert and I'm active outdoors, I occasionally suffer dehydration. In the summer, I routinely use an electrolyte replacement sold by Dr. Berg. In severe cases of dehydration, IV fluids must be given by a medial professional.

Diabetic Emergency

Diabetics are prone to episodes where their blood sugar is either too high or too low. Each condition causes a different set of problems. When blood sugar is too low, the diabetic will initially become confused, weak, and dizzy. If they are conscious and can swallow safely, the treatment of choice is to give them something to drink with sugar. A glass of orange juice is ideal. As their blood sugar decreases, they will become unconscious and may have seizures. They can become extremely sweaty and may clench their jaw tightly. Do not give an *unconscious* diabetic anything by mouth as it may be aspirated into the lungs. The safest treatment is dextrose given intravenously, which must be done by a trained medical professional.

When a diabetic's blood sugar is too high, a complex metabolic process begins that alters their blood chemistry. The primary concern is a drop in pH from ketoacidosis. This condition can be detected by characteristically sweet-smelling exhaled breath, and deep, rapid respirations. The exhaled breath of someone in ketoacidosis resembles the smell of nail polish remover. Others signs are excessive thirst (polydipsia), and excessive urination (polyuria). Many people are diagnosed with diabetes for the first time after an episode where their blood sugar is abnormally high. If the individual is fully conscious and takes insulin, they can be encouraged to administer their usual dose, but have them check their blood sugar first. A normal blood sugar reading is between 70-120. A person in diabetic ketoacidosis will usually have a blood sugar above 200. The person should be encouraged to drink fluids that do not contain sugar. Anyone with an altered mental state or signs of ketoacidosis should receive prompt medical treatment at a hospital.

How to Control Bleeding

In most cases, the body can stop bleeding on its own through a complex biochemical mechanism. To keep the discussion simple, bleeding is halted by the action of platelets. When the body is injured and starts to lose blood, platelets are released. The release of platelets causes a blood clot to form in the wound which stops the bleeding. If you must treat someone who is bleeding, here is a simple set of instructions for getting bleeding under control quickly. There are four types of bleeding you're likely to encounter; the first two will be discussed next, the third and fourth will follow later in the chapter.

The first type of bleeding is that which comes from small blood vessels located just under the skin called *capillaries*. When a small break in the skin is made, capillaries are damaged, releasing a small amount of dark red blood. It is the amount of oxygen contained in blood that determines its color. The more oxygen blood has, the brighter the color. Capillaries have lower levels of oxygen than other blood vessels, so capillary blood tends to be dark red. In healthy individuals who are not taking aspirin or blood thinners, capillary bleeding usually stops on its own in a few minutes.

The second type of bleeding comes from larger blood vessels that carry blood back to the heart. These vessels are called *veins*. The blood inside a vein has already released its oxygen to the tissues of the body, and because it has less oxygen, it is also dark red in color. When a vein is opened, it releases a larger quantity of blood than a capillary, due to its larger size. The first two types of bleeding (capillary and venous) can be treated by applying direct pressure to the wound.

Ideally, a sterile gauze dressing is placed over the wound and pressure is applied. Gauze is used because it forms a mesh web over the wound that allows platelets to aggregate, creating a blood clot that stops the flow of blood. Having a sterile dressing is nice, but it's not absolutely necessary, and in a crisis, you may not have one handy. Any clean cloth will do. Alternatives to sterile dressings are paper towels, tissues, sanitary napkins, cleaning rags, and articles of clothing.

Arrange the dressing so that it is no more than one or two layers thick. For example: a piece of paper towel folded over once or twice is all the thickness you should need. Do not make the dressing too bulky. (You'll understand why in a minute.)

Place the dressing over the wound and hold it on the wound with firm pressure for a few minutes. To check to see if the bleeding has stopped, carefully remove your hand from the dressing, leaving the dressing in place over the wound. If you can see wet blood oozing through the dressing, the bleeding has not stopped. Apply another layer of dressing material over the first one and continue applying direct pressure. DO NOT remove the dressing from the wound. If you remove the dressing, you may dislodge blood clots that formed and the bleeding will start again, requiring you to start from the beginning. This is why you should not apply a bulky dressing at the beginning. If the dressing is too thick, there is no way to check to see if the bleeding has stopped except by removing the dressing.

If the bleeding has stopped, leave the dressing in place for a few more minutes before removing it. The longer you leave it in place, the more the wound will heal and the less likely it is to begin bleeding again. If the wound is such that it may re-open after the bleeding has stopped, it may need to be closed with super glue or butterfly bandages, which is discussed below.

Dressing a Wound

Open wounds that are not covered are prone to infection. After you've stopped any bleeding, it's a judgment call whether to put a dressing over it or not. Before applying one, clean the wound gently. The best choice for cleaning a wound is povidone iodine. Other choices are hydrogen peroxide, alcohol, including isopropyl or methanol, (rum, vodka, etc.) diluted bleach, or clean water. If hydrogen peroxide or diluted bleach is used, rinse the wound with clean water afterward. After the wound has been cleaned, apply an antibiotic ointment to reduce the risk of infection.

After preparing the wound, use a sterile dressing or the cleanest piece of cloth you can find to cover it. If the dressing used to stop the bleeding was sterile, and it is not soaked with blood, consider re-using it. If you happen to have an adhesive bandage, it will make the job easier. If not, choose a suitable material. Cut it to size so that it covers the wound without hanging over too much. Secure it with whatever is available. Medical tape is ideal but it's not necessary. Elastic roller bandages work fine.

Duct tape is another option. You might use a strip of cloth torn into a long, thin strip tied around the dressing to hold it on. It doesn't need to be fancy. The goal is to keep the wound clean and covered.

NOTE: If you apply anything around an arm or leg to hold a dressing in place, be certain that it is not secured so tightly that it impairs circulation or sensation. If the individual develops skin that is red or bluish in appearance, or if you notice swelling, or if they complain of numbness or tingling in the arm or leg below the injury, it is likely that the dressing is tied or wrapped too tightly. Remove it and re-apply it, but do not secure it as tightly. Check occasionally for signs that it is too tight.

The normal way to repair a deep or long cut (laceration) to the skin is a trip to the emergency department, where the wound is cleaned and sutured closed. There are ways to do it yourself if transport to a medical facility is delayed or not possible.

Once bleeding is controlled, butterfly bandages can be applied to hold the edges of the wound closed. Before applying them, make sure the wound has been cleaned.

Super Glue

There is another way to close wounds that I discovered at a wilderness medicine conference years ago. While attending the conference, I developed a large area of dry, cracked skin on the heel of my foot. It became painful to put weight on the heel and eventually, the skin separated enough to cause bleeding. During a break between lectures, a doctor asked why I was limping. I took my sandal off and showed him the bleeding, cracked skin on my heel. He told me to go down to the hardware store and buy a couple of tubes of super glue and a bottle of peroxide. He instructed me to rinse the skin well with peroxide to kill any bacteria then dry it with a paper towel. He told me to squeeze out enough glue onto my skin to make a film that covered the entire area that was cracked. He suggested using a pencil to spread the glue around and let the glue dry, and in a few minutes, I'd be able to walk normally.

I did exactly as he instructed. A few minutes later, I couldn't tell there was any injury to the skin on my foot. The glue dried, and because it held the skin intact, the nerves under the skin were no longer being affected so the pain went away completely. The bleeding stopped immediately. In a few days, my heel was as good as new.

That was over twenty years ago. I've been a woodworker most of my life and I often cut my skin on saw blades. I've kept a tube of super glue in my shop and it's never failed to repair the cuts I've had. I've used it on my children when they had cuts. In one case, I was able to repair a full-thickness laceration to the eyebrow ridge that was several inches long, saving the person a trip to the emergency department. The wound healed perfectly in a few days and there was no scar visible.

Here's a step by step guide to repairing a skin wound using super glue:

- Apply pressure on the wound if it is bleeding, until the flow of blood is stopped. Sterile dressings are nice if you have them, but any clean piece of cloth will do. If you don't have anything made of cloth handy, don't worry. I've sometimes just held my bare hand on a wound for a few minutes until the bleeding stopped. The goal is to get the bleeding under control. Don't worry about infection yet, because we're going to disinfect the wound.

- Once the bleeding is reasonably controlled, the next step is to clean it. Always be sure to clean a wound thoroughly before applying super glue. Anything that is in the wound before the glue is applied will stay there afterward, including bacteria. The biggest risk with broken skin is not bleeding to death, but infection. If you have povidone iodine available, use it to clean the wound. If you don't have povidone iodine, hydrogen peroxide can be used but be aware that it destroys living tissue including human skin. If it is used for cleaning the wound, rinse it off with water after 30 seconds.

- Super glue will adhere better to dry skin. If you happen to have a sterile dressing available, you can use it to dry the area. The goal is only to dry the skin *around* the wound, not to dry the *inside* of the wound itself. Always avoid touching the inside of the wound with anything once it has been cleaned.

- Now, it's time to apply the glue. You don't want to apply the glue into the open wound. The goal is to bring together the edges of broken skin into the most normal alignment possible so the wound is closed. (If you have someone who can assist, ask them to help you. This part is easier done with two people.) Being careful not to touch the inside of the wound, close the wound, by pinching the skin together and at the same time, apply a ribbon of super glue to the entire edge of the wound. If you notice any part of the wound where the glue did not cover the skin, apply a little glue to that area. The goal is to completely cover the open edges of skin. Allow the glue to dry for a minute or so before releasing the skin.

- If the wound is such that the skin cannot be brought together to close it up, another option is creating a thin layer of glue over the entire area, essentially making a temporary artificial patch. In time, the body will heal itself and the wound will develop a scab, then a normal layer of skin will appear.

- Be extremely careful when using super glue near the eyes. Super glue can be very thin and it runs quickly downhill. It will glue an eyelid shut in a matter of seconds. If you must use it near the eyes, a thicker glue is preferable. Consider purchasing one with a gel consistency. When using near the eyes, tilt the person's head so that any excess glue will run away from the eyes and nose, not toward them.

- Be careful not to touch anything that has fresh super glue on it as the glue bonds skin in seconds and it will bond your fingers together if you're not careful. Super glue generally wears off in a few days. Allow it to remain on the skin until it wears off by itself.

- If the wound shows signs of infection, like redness, tenderness, discharge of pus, or if you develop a fever, you probably have an infected wound. The treatment is the same. You'll have to open the wound and clean it well before closing it again with super glue. A disposable scalpel is ideal for this, but a clean, small knife can be used. Once the wound is opened, control any bleeding. Use povidone iodine or peroxide to clean it. If peroxide is used, rinse it off and dry the wound with a sterile dressing. I've had several lacerations that I closed with super glue that became infected a few days later. In each case, it was because I failed to properly clean the wound before applying the glue. If you clean it well before closing it, infection should not be a problem.

NOTE: Super glue is a modern medical marvel. Surgeons began using it in the operating room around the time I first heard about it. You can buy medical grade super glue, but regular super glue works just as well and can be bought for a few dollars at hardware and discount stores. There are different thicknesses available from thin to a thick gel. You might experiment with them and pick the one that works best for you. Super glue is typically sold in tubes that contain less than 1/10th of an ounce. Although larger bottles are available, some prefer the small tubes as the glue inside the container can harden and dry after they're opened, making them single use items.

Life-Threatening Bleeding

The third type of bleeding is that which occurs when an artery is opened. Arteries are the blood vessels that supply oxygenated blood from the heart to the body. Because it carries more oxygen than other blood vessels, arterial blood is bright red in color. Because it is under higher pressure than other vessels, arterial bleeding can appear as a steady stream of bright red blood that squirts. If you've never seen arterial bleeding in person, it can be dramatic. Arterial bleeding is an immediate threat to life. If it is not stopped quickly, death will follow in a matter of seconds.

Controlling arterial bleeding requires you to do a couple of things in quick succession. They can be illustrated in the following story of a patient I transported years ago.

The patient was involved in a street fight during a night of rioting. The rioting caused a lot of injuries and property damage, including the destruction of a police cruiser that was flipped over and set on fire. Our patient was not a rioter. He tried to break up a fight when he was thrown through a store-front window and suffered deep lacerations to both upper arms.

When I arrived on scene and saw the bright red blood flowing from both of his arms, I quickly placed one hand on each of the wounds and applied the firmest pressure I could. I never let go of his arms from the moment I made contact with him. My partner got help loading the patient on the gurney. With me applying firm pressure to the patient's arms, we drove as fast as we could to the nearest hospital. My partner needed help to unload the gurney at the hospital. We rolled the patient into the emergency department with me still clinging to his arms. The attending doctor asked what the injuries were. I told him the patient had arterial bleeding from lacerations to both upper arms from being thrown through a window. I told him I thought we should to go immediately to surgery. The doctor didn't believe me and wanted to inspect the patient's arms for himself. I let off pressure slightly on one arm and a bright red pool of blood formed on the gurney. The doctor then decided to take the patient directly to surgery. **TIP:** Although it may be tempting to observe a protest or riot, being in the area as an innocent bystander can make you a victim like this man was. When civil unrest breaks out, move to a safe location.

Stopping Severe Bleeding

You must work quickly with a person who has arterial or major venous bleeding. You may not be able to tell the difference between the two and it doesn't matter which one you're dealing with. The treatment for severe arterial and venous bleeding is the same. If you act quickly, you can get the bleeding under control, but if you don't, the individual will die. The reality is that even if you get the bleeding under control, without surgery, they may die anyway. Although I was able to control the bleeding of the patient I described above, I had no ability to repair the damage, and without surgery or a miracle, he would have died. With severe bleeding, the odds of survival without surgery are poor.

There are two approaches to controlling severe bleeding. The first method is to apply direct pressure to the wound, which we've already discussed. In the case of my patient above, I held direct pressure as long as I could without letting go until he was in surgery. Direct pressure on the injury is your first and best option. If direct pressure is not working and the patient continues to bleed despite your efforts, the only other option is to apply a tourniquet.

Some people are under the impression that the application of a tourniquet is the best treatment to stop life-threatening bleeding. I worked as a paramedic for 35 years and never had to apply one. That's not to say I never encountered patients with severe arterial bleeding. I have. But the application of direct pressure is a better option than a tourniquet because it doesn't cut off blood flow to the affected limb. A tourniquet should be considered a last resort and not a first line treatment.

WARNING: The application of a tourniquet is a life and death matter. It cuts off blood flow to the entire limb below where it is placed. In a matter of hours, tissue death occurs and the limb will eventually die, requiring amputation. Once applied, the individual should seek medical attention as soon as possible. The complications following the application of a tourniquet are many and they can cause prolonged illness or death.

Here are instructions for applying a tourniquet

- A tourniquet can only be applied to an arm or leg. You'll need some kind of material that can be secured tightly in a band around the arm or leg. The ideal material is a triangular bandage. A leather or fabric belt, or a piece of cloth torn into a strip two to three inches wide will work. Other choices are a nylon tie-down strap, a guitar strap, a strap from a backpack or camera bag, or even a bungee cord. Any similar cord or strap may work. In an emergency, you'll have to improvise with whatever you have available and do it quickly. Alternatively, a commercially made tourniquet can be purchased and kept in a first aid kit.

- Place the tourniquet around the injured limb about an inch or two above the location of the injury site (closer to the heart). Tighten the tourniquet so that it is tight enough to stop the flow of blood. One method commonly used to tighten a tourniquet is to slip a long, thin object like a stick underneath the tourniquet, parallel to the limb. Rotate the stick in a circular motion and as you do, the tourniquet will begin to twist around the stick and tighten. When the tourniquet is tightened so that the bleeding is controlled, secure it with tape or another device to prevent it from loosening again. After a tourniquet has been applied, write the time it was applied on the person's skin in ink. This information must be given to the medical team that takes over care.

Internal Bleeding

This section will help you assess the fourth type of bleeding, which is internal. The ability of modern medical practitioners to correctly diagnose internal bleeding is heavily dependent on expensive imaging technology. CT scans have been the gold standard for diagnostic testing for many years. But in a crisis, their availability is not guaranteed and some forms of internal bleeding can be identified without medical imaging. For that reason, I'll give you a review of common sources of internal bleeding along with the symptoms they cause to help you determine the most likely causes of bleeding.

NOTE: Please consider this information as a set of basic principles, and not a reliable diagnostic tool. Medical imaging, blood testing, and examination by a specialist should always be considered the best course of action when you suspect internal bleeding. This information is not intended to replace standard diagnostic testing and treatment. It is provided in case they are unavailable.

Internal bleeding, like any other type of bleeding, is usually self-limiting. The body of a normal, healthy individual can stop bleeding on its own. But there are a few reasons why bleeding may become persistent or severe enough to require medical treatment. The use of blood thinners like aspirin, coumadin, and the use of NSAIDS like ibuprofen, are a common cause of internal bleeding. While these drugs provide certain benefits, they have the side-effect of increased bleeding.

Bleeding Into the Brain

The brain is an organ rich with blood vessels. When blood vessels in the brain rupture—whether due to trauma or spontaneously—the bleeding is normally limited because the skull is a closed box. It only has so much space available and bleeding, once it has filled the available space, usually halts. The volume of blood that can normally be lost into the skull is very small and is not enough to cause death from a loss of blood. Nevertheless, thousands of people die every year from bleeding into the brain. Death does not result from a loss of blood, but from the disruption of the normal brain activity when blood clots displace brain tissue.

Symptoms of bleeding into the brain are numerous. They are nearly identical to the symptoms of a brain tumor and until a CT scan or MRI is done, it is usually impossible to know for certain which is the culprit.

Intracranial bleeding (blood loss inside the skull) may happen spontaneously or after a blow to the head. The usual symptoms are a severe headache, (often described as the worst headache of their life) confusion, babbling speech or the inability to speak, poor muscle coordination, paralysis or near paralysis on one or both sides of the face or body, inability to walk, sudden blindness, and seizures. If the individual has one normal sized pupil while the other pupil is noticeably larger, it's a sign of a possible head injury. The classic progression of symptoms for a *subarachnoid* bleed are a blow to the head followed by a brief loss of consciousness. The individual regains consciousness only to slowly become less alert over the next 24 to 48 hours, eventually becoming unresponsive. All these symptoms can be associated with some type of bleeding into the brain and aside from surgical intervention, there is little you can do for this condition. If someone displays signs of intracranial bleeding, they should seek immediate medical attention.

Bleeding into the Chest
The chest cavity contains blood vessels that bring blood to and from the heart and lungs. Bleeding in the chest is usually due to the rupture of one of these blood vessels and can be life-threatening. Bleeding into the chest is usually due to either a blunt or a penetrating injury. A blunt injury is one that does not break the integrity of the chest wall. Blunt injuries may leave a skin abrasion or bruise and may involve broken ribs or broken bones in the spine, but the inner lining of the chest cavity is not broken. Examples are being punched or hit with a baseball bat in the ribs. A penetrating injury breaks the integrity of the chest wall. Examples are knife and bullet wounds.

Internal bleeding in the chest is common after an assault, car accident, traumatic injury, being shot with a gun, or being

stabbed in the chest with a sharp instrument. Upon examination, you may notice a large bruise on the back, chest, or
ribs and there may be severe pain. More serious symptoms
are increasing shortness of breath, pale or bluish skin color,
coughing up blood, and unconsciousness. Significant bleeding—
whether internal or external—is usually accompanied by fast
heart rate and low blood pressure. Chest injuries usually cause
pulse oximetry levels to drop. Internal bleeding in the chest is
a life-threatening situation and medical help must be found or
the individual is likely to die.

If someone has sustained a penetrating chest injury, look
for and control any external bleeding with a dressing or clean
cloth. Look for air bubbles coming from the wound. If bubbles
are noted, it's because air is being sucked into the chest cavity
through the wound. Air that enters the chest through a wound
becomes trapped outside the lungs, and it displaces air contained in the lungs. The opening in the skin must be sealed or
the person's lung(s) may collapse. To seal an open chest wound,
cut a square piece of plastic wrap larger than the wound and
tape it in place over the wound being sure to seal the edges so
air cannot get into the wound. A gloved hand placed over the
wound will seal it temporarily until plastic wrap can be applied.
If you happen to have a bag-valve-mask or pocket mask, you
can use it to assist respirations. If you have a supply of medical
grade oxygen and a way to deliver it, you should do so while
transporting the person to a hospital.

Abdominal Bleeding

While the chest has a nicely designed cage of bones to protect
the vital organs inside it, the abdomen does not. The abdomen is
more vulnerable to bleeding due to blunt injury than the chest.
There are many organs in the abdomen. Some like the spleen
are full of blood vessels that can bleed, but some like the gall-
bladder, have few blood vessels.

Internal bleeding in the abdomen can result from blunt or
penetrating injury, the same as with injuries to the chest. Signs

and symptoms are severe pain, tenderness, and bruising. One worrisome sign is the tendency to "guard" the abdomen. When the individual with abdominal pain senses that someone is going to touch them, they will put a hand in the way to prevent you from touching them. Often the only position of comfort they can find is to curl up in a ball. The abdomen is normally flat and soft to the touch. Signs of possible internal bleeding are an abdomen that is hard to the touch or distended to larger than normal size. Bruising is another sign as is pain that radiates from the abdomen to the shoulder.

Some internal bleeding is found when using the toilet. Blood in your urine may be a sign of bleeding in the kidneys or bladder. Blood in your stool indicates bleeding somewhere in the digestive tract. Blood in the stool can take on different appearances. Sometimes the blood appears as normal, reddish in color, and it may be clotted. But blood can also appear to be black and have the appearance of tar or it can appear like coffee grounds.

Here's a way to know where the blood is coming from based on its appearance.

Blood that is bright red in color has not been altered by enzymes in the digestive tract. This blood comes from somewhere near the rectum and if it is predominantly found on the toilet paper itself, it is often the result of hemorrhoids. Blood that is darker red in color, but is still recognizable as blood often comes from the colon.

Blood that appears as black, tarry, or has a foul smell (melena) has been altered by enzymes in the digestive tract. This kind of bleeding usually originates high in the digestive tract, and is often seen with a stomach ulcer. Vomiting blood is another sign of internal bleeding. When the vomit has the appearance of coffee grounds, it usually indicates a bleed high in the digestive tract and is often due to an ulcer of the stomach or esophagus.

Pelvic Bleeding

The pelvis, like the chest, is protected by a bony cage and bleeding in the pelvis is often due to blunt or penetrating injuries. Common signs are severe pain, bruising, tenderness, guarding, and a distended appearance. In the case of blunt injury like a fall or car accident, you might notice a grating sound as broken pelvic bones rub against one another. Pelvic fractures are very painful and they can damage the vessels that carry blood to and from the legs. Blood loss into the abdomen and pelvis can be severe enough to cause death.

Most causes of internal bleeding require surgical treatment, though some may resolve on their own, and a few can be treated at home. Hemorrhoids can be frightening, but they're not usually a serious problem. Blood in the urine can come from a kidney stone and if the stone passes, the bleeding usually stops. Stomach ulcers can often be treated with over the counter remedies. Again, I would advise you to seek medical help in most cases as internal bleeding can often be a life-threatening problem.

A Basic First Aid Kit

A first aid kit can be assembled with items such as a few disposable gloves, a triangular bandage, two rolls of tape (3M makes brand called Transpore that is a good all-purpose tape), an assortment of Band-Aids, butterfly bandages, two inch wide roller bandages, a few rolls of Coban (an elastic, adhesive material), some 2x2 inch, and 4x4 inch wide sterile gauze pads, scissors, a tube of super glue, a few iodine prep pads, a disposable scalpel, and a tube of antibiotic ointment. (These items can be purchased at a pharmacy or online.)

It's difficult to stockpile prescription medications because only limited amounts can be prescribed without violating the law. Commonly, medications are prescribed to provide a one-month supply, but some physicians will write a prescription to cover a 90-day period. Try to have prescriptions filled so that you'll have the longest window of time between refills. For non-prescription medications and supplements, have enough on hand to last at least 90 days.

15

Surviving Nuclear War

THE INFORMATION IN THIS CHAPTER may be difficult for some to accept because it will conflict with their beliefs about nuclear war. Movies, our education system, politicians, and the media have conditioned us to think that nuclear war is equivalent to the destruction of mankind. What if I told you there is a high probability that more than 90 percent of the world's population would survive a nuclear war? I'll provide information to support this assertion. If my proposition is true, does it not require us to prepare for the aftermath of a nuclear exchange?

During the Cold War, it was feared that the U.S. and the Soviet Union might use nuclear weapons in an all-out exchange that would lead to mutually assured destruction of both countries and much of the world. Such an exchange never occurred. But the assumption that nuclear war is equivalent to the destruction of mankind persists despite changes in the way nuclear weapons are used.

When we mention nuclear weapons, most people think of nuclear-capable intercontinental ballistic missiles (ICBMs). During the Cold War, tactical nuclear weapons that could be deployed on the battlefield did not exist. They exist today, and they're deployed in ways similar to how conventional munitions are used, and they do not cause widespread devastation. And in fact, neither do the warheads delivered by most ICBMs.

E.J Mendoza is a research nuclear physicist who wrote a book titled *Gearing Up for Surviving a Nuclear War*. In his book, Dr. Mendoza describes the damage that would be inflicted by the detonation of a typical medium-sized Russian nuclear bomb—an 800-kiloton warhead. Mendoza writes: "The fireball from such a detonation would reach a radius of 1.5 kilometers and cover about 4.15 kilometers. Within this fireball radius, all buildings would be destroyed entirely, and all human life instantly vaporized." He continues: "Within a blast radius of about 2 km, almost all buildings will collapse, killing most or all of the people inside. Within the thermal radius of 9 km, victims will suffer third-degree burns that would require intensive medical attention to survive. Anyone surviving the burns and blast damage within about a 2.5 km radius would be exposed to intense ionizing radiation, sufficient to eventually cause almost certain death." Mendoza then writes: "Beyond the radius of the thermal burn zone, physical damage to structures and human bodies is limited and fairly minor. That leaves one more aspect to discuss:... radioactive fallout."

Fallout refers to the radioactive byproducts of a nuclear explosion, including both unstable radioactive elements produced by the atomic chain reaction, as well as matter such as dirt, ash, and pulverized building material that has been both irradiated and thrown up into the air by the force of the explosion. It is so called because the radioactive particles become suspended in the atmosphere and then later "fall out" as rain, dew, or other atmospheric deposits, as they form the nuclei of water droplets created from atmospheric vapor. The decay rates of radioactive elements in fallout range from hours to weeks. Substances having the shorter half-lives will pose the most intense and immediate risk to human health because of their relatively high energy output. The deposition of fallout is obviously most intense in the area closely surrounding the nuclear explosion itself as the downdraft from the atomic heat reaction blows irradiated particles down toward the ground, and they suffuse the immediate vicinity. However, the atmospheric suspension of the particles leads to their migration by way of wind currents, meaning that depending on meteorological conditions at the time of the explosion and subsequent to it, the fallout can spread far afield, even ascending into the high stratosphere, and be deposited many weeks later in areas quite far from the initial blast site.

On the issue of delayed exposure to radioactive fallout, Mendoza notes: "People caught in the open in the immediate vicinity of a nuclear explosion can be exposed to doses as high as 30 Gray, sufficient to cause intense cellular damage, leading to immediate severe sickness and probable death within months, even with immediate medical attention. Those who are farther away but caught within the fallout plume within two weeks of the explosion can be exposed to a dose of up to 3.5 Gray, which can be sufficient to cause permanent disability even if medical attention is obtained. Getting into a protected shelter where you can avoid contact with the fallout for this critical period and using protective hazmat gear is essential to avoiding the effects of radiation sickness."

Note that Mendoza gives a two-week window during which exposure to radiation is potentially hazardous following a nuclear detonation. Why two weeks?

Mendoza explains: "The toxic effects of nuclear fallout drop quickly with time due to relatively quick decomposition of the most intensely radioactive byproducts. The general rule of thumb for calculating the toxicity of radioactive fallout is called the "7-10 rule," which states that for every factor of seven in time passed since the blast, the ionizing radiation output of the resulting fallout will reduce by a factor of 10. Therefore, after 7 hours, the level of radiation emitted by the fallout has reduced to 10% of its original strength; and after 49 (7x7) hours, it has reduced to 1%; and then, after just over two weeks, it has reduced to 0.1%. This is the point at which it is widely considered safe for decontamination of fallout areas to commence and people who have sheltered from nuclear fallout to emerge from their sequestration. However, low-level radioactive contamination can linger in the environment for many years after the explosion and cause an increased risk of cancer, necessitating continual detoxification if one wishes to maintain good health."

Next, we want to know the probability that a given population will survive a nuclear attack. Allow me to provide a hypothetical situation that calculates the approximate percentage of people that would likely survive one. I live in Phoenix, Arizona. The metropolitan area of Phoenix has a population of approximately 5 million people distributed throughout Maricopa County, which covers an area of 9,224 square miles. Let's imagine that not one, but three medium-sized Russian warheads make it through the U.S. missile defense system and detonate in or near the city of Phoenix.

Using Dr. Mendoza's numbers, the immediate area where life will no longer exist due to a nuclear explosion has a radius of approximately 9 kilometers or roughly 5 miles. That equates to 100 square miles per warhead. If we multiply 100 square miles by 3 (the number of warheads in our scenario), we arrive at 300 square miles where life and buildings would be eradicated. This would leave 97 percent of Maricopa County's 9,224 square miles physically intact. Of course, airborne radiated particles will continue to cause harm for several weeks, but the major brunt of the immediate blast is much smaller than many people might imagine.

The website NUKEMAP (https://nuclearsecrecy.com/nuke-map/) allows users to select a geographic location and the size of a nuclear warhead to simulate the damage caused by a detonation. Using the simulator, when an 800-kiloton warhead is detonated at random locations in the Phoenix area, each strike averages roughly 150,000 deaths. The detonation of three 800-kiloton warheads might take the lives of 450,000-500,000 people and leave more than 1 million people injured. I don't know how realistic it is to imagine that three nuclear warheads would be detonated in one city. It would seem (at least to me) to be a worst-case scenario. Still, 90 percent of the population would remain alive following such an attack.

Nuclear Winter – Fact or Fiction?

In the 1980s, scientists began speculating about the possibility that soot and smoke from fires caused by nuclear war might remain aloft in the atmosphere and block out the sunlight. The term "nuclear winter" was coined in 1983 by Richard Turco in reference to a computer model he developed that projected that after a large-scale nuclear war, massive quantities of soot and smoke would remain aloft in the air for years, causing a severe planet-wide drop in temperature which might lead to catastrophic crop failure. It has been theorized that due to changes in climate, billions of people would die in the years that followed a nuclear war.

The theory was put to the test in 1991 during the Kuwaiti oil fires. Scientists like Carl Sagan predicted that soot from the fires would reach altitudes of around 40,000 feet, remain aloft for more a year, and lead to world-wide temperature changes. In 1992, data was analyzed that found minimal atmospheric effects from the fires in Kuwait. The temperature did change a few degrees but it was limited to the Persian Gulf region and it was temporary. Smoke plumes reached about 10,000 feet in altitude and soot remained in the atmosphere for a few days before being removed by rain. The nuclear winter hypothesis lost the support of many in the scientific community, though the narrative is still popular today among non-scientists. It is this author's opinion that nuclear winter does not pose a real threat to our existence.

Rather than being the end of civilization, a nuclear war would mean the beginning of a different way of life for the 90 percent that survives. Since most people will survive, it's worth spending some time making plans for life after a nuclear exchange.

If you have access to potassium iodide at the time of a radiologic emergency, consider taking it. Radioactive iodine can be released in a nuclear detonation. Uptake of this compound can lead to thyroid cancer. Taking potassium iodide can saturate the thyroid so it doesn't absorb radioactive iodine. Potassium iodide can be purchased over the counter. The adult and teen dose is 135 mg at the time of exposure and another 135 mg four hours later. For children ages 3-12, the dose is 65 mg at the time of exposure and another 65 mg four hours later.

Dr. Mendoza prescribes a simple course of action to survive the two-week window during which coming into contact with toxic fallout can be deadly. He recommends sheltering in place. If you are outside when a nuclear bomb detonates near you, immediately get inside your home. Seek shelter in another building if you're not at home at the time of detonation. If you live near the blast zone, especially if you're downwind of it, tape plastic film over the heating and air conditioning vent openings in your home. Seal the edges of doors and windows with tape, and turn off the heat and air conditioning system to avoid bringing contaminated dirt and dust into your home. After two to three hours, remove the plastic film and tape, but do not turn on the heat or AC yet. Leaving the tape in place for more than five hours puts you at risk of asphyxiation.

Mendoza advises remaining in your home for two weeks until the most dangerous radioactive particles have had time to decay. If you've stored food, water, and other necessities, now is the time to savor the fruits of your labor. After two weeks, you can turn on your home's heating and air conditioning system and begin venturing out to assess the local situation, but consider wearing a disposable Tyvek suit, shoe covers, goggles, and gloves to avoid coming into contact with contaminated particles. (These items are inexpensive and can be purchased at a hardware store or online retail outlets.) If you're adequately supplied and not overly curious, you can remain in your home even longer.

Mendoza's guidance creates a catch 22 for those who live in locations with extreme temperatures. If you live in a cold climate, do you turn on the heating system to prevent freezing to death and risk introducing radiation into your home? The same predicament exists if you live in an extremely hot climate where air conditioning is needed. I can't offer a solution to that dilemma other than to suggest asking God to provide you with one. (The solution could involve supernatural control of the weather, which will be discussed in a later chapter.)

Upon returning home, remove the hazmat items while you're outside and leave them in a container for reuse. Do not bring potentially contaminated items into your home.

When coming into contact with dirt or dust that is potentially contaminated, take a shower and wash yourself well. Scrub your hair and scalp and any facial hair you may have thoroughly. Hand sanitizer will not remove contaminated particles. Use soap. If you've breathed in dust or dirt, forcefully blow it out your nose or cough it out. If you have family members, have them do the same. If you have pets, wash them with soap and water. If your water service has not been disrupted, you might consider routinely showering after returning home in the months after a nuclear blast. If your water supply has been disrupted, you can use a solar shower, but be sure to use water from an uncontaminated source. Pool and pond water are likely to be contaminated following a nuclear detonation. Do not eat or drink anything outside of your home that is not from a sealed container or package. Anything in an open container may be contaminated. If you can avoid contamination from radioactive particles for two weeks after the blast, you can survive the immediate event. Preventing contamination in the months that follow will increase your odds of long-term survival.

EMP

The detonation of a nuclear bomb creates a strong electromagnetic pulse (EMP) capable of destroying the electronic circuits of radios, televisions, phones, computers, and other electronic devices. An EMP can also ruin the control module of cars with electronic ignition. How does an EMP damage electronic devices? By introducing voltage and current surges into circuits that are higher than what they are designed to handle.

The risk of being affected by an EMP strike depends on the size of the device, the altitude at which it is detonated, and one's distance from the detonation. The intensity of an electromagnetic wave decreases proportional to the square of distance. Thus, a low altitude detonation releases an intense wave of electromagnetic energy over a small area. A high-altitude blast disperses the same energy over a larger area. Some experts speculate that most of the U.S. would be significantly affected by an EMP detonated 250 miles above the earth, but it's difficult to know with certainty how widespread the damage might be.

Damaging electromagnetic radiation can also be released during an extremely strong solar storm. We can protect electronic devices by shielding them in a material resistant to the waves created by an EMP. Typically, this is done with metallic screens and metal enclosures called Faraday Cages. Any essential electronic device that you want to protect from an EMP should be enclosed in some type of protective barrier. The problem is that since one never knows when an EMP will occur, the device should always remain in the protected enclosure to be effective. This means it will not be available for daily use. One solution is to purchase duplicate devices: one is used as needed, and the other is stored in a protective enclosure.

Geiger Counter

Following a nuclear detonation, a Geiger counter can be used to evaluate water, food, and other items to determine if they are contaminated with radiation.

There exists the possibility of a government operation designed to compel citizens to self-quarantine for a lengthy period under the false belief that a nuclear emergency exists. A conventional bomb could be detonated, and the public could be falsely informed that it was a nuclear event perpetrated by a foreign adversary. Or the government could falsely claim a low-yield "dirty bomb" was detonated. Since few people have the equipment needed to detect the presence of radiation, they would not know they were being deceived. Geiger counters can be purchased from many retail outlets. Having one and knowing how to use it correctly would give one the information they need to assess if a radiologic emergency was real or imagined.

16

Satellite Communication

SEVERAL OF THE CRISES WE'VE examined thus far could cause us to lose access to phone and internet. The chapters that follow explore alternate means of communication. Internet and cellular phones are convenient ways to communicate. The alternatives are less popular because each has disadvantages. The pros and cons of each alternative will be highlighted to help you make informed decisions about their usefulness.

One option for communication when internet and cellular services are not available is a device that connects to a satellite network. A personal locator beacon (PLB) is a satellite-linked device that, when activated, sends a distress signal to nearby search and rescue units. Typically used for mountaineering, they can be used in other emergencies, but caution should be exercised. PLBs should only be activated in an actual emergency.

For years, two-way satellite communication required buying a phone and paying for a monthly data plan. Satellite phones and data plans can be cost-prohibitive. In 2022, top-tier Apple iPhones offered satellite communication for emergencies. The service is not available for messaging friends and family. It only works if your phone does not have wireless or cellular service. It allows you to send and receive text messages with emergency services near you. When used with an app, it can send your location to people in your emergency contact list.

In 2023, Qualcomm announced that it would partner with Iridium to offer Android phones that connect to a satellite network to provide similar services. Samsung announced it will soon offer phones with satellite connectivity. So far, phone manufacturers are only aiming to provide connection to emergency services. Off-grid communication with friends and family is not an option.

Satellite communication with friends and family via smartphone is available with a device that connects to a satellite network. These devices are sold by Zoleo, Bivy Stick, Garmin, and other manufacturers. They connect to a smartphone or tablet by Bluetooth and a mobile app. The communicator sends text or email messages composed on the app over a satellite network.

The Zoleo communicator allows text or email messages to be sent to any email address or phone number that has service, even if the receiving party is not on the Zoleo network. When a message is sent, the device will first try to send it over a cellular or wireless network. If one is not available, it will be sent over the satellite network. Since charges are incurred for each message sent, this reduces monthly costs. Zoleo's monthly plans start at $20 per month. Once a user has had a paid monthly plan for three months, the plan can be paused indefinitely for $4 per month and restarted at any time.

It may sound like a bomb-proof solution, but there may be a fly in the ointment. Satellite communicators receive messages from a user who may not have internet or cellular access. The communicator sends a signal directly to a satellite. So far, so good. If the entire message chain were space-based, there would be no problem during a terrestrial internet disruption. But if, at any point, the message must go through a ground-based internet gateway, an internet outage that affects that gateway would render this option unusable. I spoke with a Zoleo technical support assistant who confirmed their system does use ground-based servers to handle messaging traffic. The assistant could not state confidently that their service would be available during a widespread internet outage. The availability of satellite service would seem to depend on how widespread the internet outage is. If traffic from an affected area could be rerouted to an unaffected area, messages may go through. When cellular carriers are not able to provide service, satellite communicators are a good alternative, but it is unclear just how reliable they would be during a widespread internet outage.

Satellite Internet

Many people have switched to satellite internet service providers like Starlink. Some believe that satellite internet service will be available when other internet providers don't have service. As popular as this idea is, it has a major flaw. Although the end user receives their internet data via satellite, that data passes through the same ground-based servers used by all internet providers. Until satellite internet providers can host their own servers in space, their services will be susceptible to the same problems as other providers.

One issue with satellite, cellular, and internet services is that the end user doesn't control the network. While it's convenient to use a communication network someone else maintains, the availability of service is completely dependent on others. In a crisis where communication networks are not available, its preferable to have equipment that you control. That is where our discussion turns to the use of radios.

The following chapters on radio operations contain a fair amount of technical information. I've tried to avoid discussions of highly technical or esoteric subjects. When technical information is presented, it will be brief, and an explanation will be given to help the novice understand it. Some readers will find the technical information useful, but others will not. Consider these chapters to be reference material. If you do not need this information now, you may wish to come back to it later. That said, I think it would be wise to gather some of this equipment now, even if you do not intend to use it immediately.

17

Radio Basics

THE INFORMATION PRESENTED IN THE following chapters is highly detailed. In some cases, I've included the precise steps one should take to operate certain devices. I've done this because finding such instruction by wading through owner's manuals, watching videos, and exploring online forums is tedious work and such information may not be available in a grid-down crisis. If you find yourself needing to know how to operate a particular piece of equipment in a hurry, you'll be glad to have the information included in this book. Following the chapters that describe specific radios, you'll find a reference guide to help you decide which radio to use in a particular situation.

There are two basic types of radios. Some radios allow for listening while others allow you to transmit messages. With the exception of the chapter, "Listening Only," the discussions that follow refer to radios capable of both receiving and transmitting messages in some manner.

Radios transmit a signal by creating a wave of electromagnetic energy. The wave of energy travels through the atmosphere and can be received by another radio. Radios transmit electromagnetic waves of different lengths. Some radio waves are short, while others are long. These waves have both peaks and troughs. As a wave moves, it oscillates between the high and low points. Radio waves oscillate at different speeds. Some waves oscillate slowly, while others oscillate quickly. The speed at which a radio wave oscillates is called its *frequency*. Radio frequency (RF) is measured in *hertz*. One hertz equals a radio wave completing one positive and one negative phase in one second. A wave that oscillates one hundred times per second is assigned a frequency of 100 hertz. A wave that oscillates 1,000 times per second is assigned the frequency of one kilohertz. A wave that oscillates at one million cycles per second is assigned a frequency of one megahertz.

Radio Bands

Regulatory agencies set aside dozens of segments of the radio spectrum for use by certain groups of people. These segments of the radio spectrum are known as *bands*. A radio band is a narrow range of frequencies. One band includes frequencies between 50-54 megahertz. Although technically, a band is a range of frequencies, it is sometimes identified by one frequency within that range. This particular band is known as the 50 megahertz band. Because the length of a radio wave in this band is six meters long, it is also known as the 6 meter band. Another commonly used band is the 70 centimeter band,- so-named because a wave on this band is roughly 70 centimeters long. This band includes frequencies from 420-450 megahertz.

Most portable radios used for two way communication transmit on segments of the radio spectrum designated as very high frequency (VHF) and ultrahigh-frequency (UHF). The VHF spectrum runs from 30-300 megahertz. The UHF spectrum includes frequencies between 300-3,000 megahertz (3 Gigahertz). Some radios transmit on multiple bands. Some transmit on only one. In the U.S., the Federal Communications Commission (FCC) regulates what frequencies can be used for radio transmissions and the power limitations for each band.

Line of Sight

Radios capable of two-way communication are used by operators who alternate sending and receiving signals. A radio that transmits and receives signals is sometimes called a *transceiver*. A transceiver may also be called a *station*. Most radio waves in the VHF and UHF spectrum do not travel far between listening stations. They're limited to the terrain that can be seen by line of sight or the distance between horizons. At sea level, the horizon is roughly three miles away due to the curvature of the earth. As the surface of the earth curves, radio signals (with a few exceptions) travel in a straight direction. Let's imagine two stations that are 15 miles apart and are at sea level. One station sends a signal in the direction of the other one. After traveling a few miles toward the receiving station, as the surface of the earth curves below it, the signal will move into the upper atmosphere above the listening station. VHF and UHF radio waves at ground level can be expected to travel approximately three miles in any direction before traveling off into space. The geographic area in which a radio signal can be received by a listening station is called the *radio horizon*. Line of sight communication is also affected by trees, buildings, hills, and other objects that reflect or absorb signals. While theoretically, the range of a radio might be three miles, when trees, buildings and other obstructions are accounted for, the real-world range may be only one mile.

In summary, a portable radio used at ground level with a stock antenna has an effective range of less than 10 miles. Such radios are suitable for off-grid use over short distances, i.e., at the neighborhood, city, or county level. Communication over longer distances (over the horizon) on UHF and VHF bands is possible by employing one of several methods, which will be discussed shortly.

18

Listening Only

IN A CRISIS, IT'S ESSENTIAL to have information. When internet and cell phone services are unavailable, we must find an alternate way of gathering it. We can do that by listening to public broadcasts and emergency responder radio traffic.

AM and FM Radio

Some AM and FM radio stations have emergency backup power. During a crisis where cellular or internet service is not available, these stations should be able to provide information about the severity and duration of a crisis. Metropolitan areas typically have stations that are designated as emergency broadcast stations that provide the public information during a crisis. It would be wise to find out in advance which stations near you are designated as emergency broadcast stations. Write down their frequencies and keep them with other important information. Most vehicles have AM and FM radios, though some newer models may not have AM radio service. **TIP:** Many handheld radios designed for use by amateur radio operators, such as the Baofeng UV-5R, can receive FM broadcast stations.

Scanners

A scanner is type of radio that can be used to listen to law enforcement, fire, and emergency service dispatchers and responders. Scanners do not transmit signals. Whether a scanner will receive radio traffic in your area depends on the type of radios used by public safety agencies. Some public agencies use radios that can be heard with a scanner, but many have switched to encrypted radios. Traffic on these radios cannot be scanned. Radio traffic that is encoded, but not encrypted can be heard with a scanner capable of decoding the signals. Before purchasing a scanner, find out what type of radios are used by the agencies in your area whose traffic you want to listen to. You should also decide whether you want to transmit messages in a crisis. Some handheld radio transmitters also have scanning capabilities. You could scan local emergency traffic and transmit using a single radio. Prices for handheld scanners begin at $25. Models capable of scanning encoded radio traffic can cost as much as $650.

Weather Broadcasts

In the U.S., you can listen to NOAA weather broadcasts with a radio capable of receiving one of seven channels within the frequency range of 162.400 through 162.550 MHz, collectively known as the weather band. The frequencies are 162.400 MHz, 162.425 MHz, 162.450 MHz, 162.475 MHz, 162.500 MHz, 162.525 MHz, and 162.550 MHz.

Shortwave Listening

Hundreds of radio stations across the globe broadcast news, weather, and entertainment by transmitting signals that skip off the atmosphere, which are received by listeners thousands of miles away. (We will discuss this phenomenon in more detail in later chapters.) Many of these stations will be on the air during a grid-down emergency. You can stay abreast of current events if you have a shortwave radio capable of receiving these transmissions. Shortwave radios are not capable of transmitting voice messages, but they can receive them.

An inexpensive multi-band radio can receive transmissions from local AM and FM broadcast stations, weather channels and shortwave stations. A radio requires a power source, and the usual power supply may not be available in an emergency. Kaito's Voyager line of radios can be powered by a solar panel, hand crank, a home power outlet, and batteries. Some models come with a USB charger and 12-volt adapter.

C.Crane and Tecsun make more sophisticated shortwave listening radios that offer a broader range of frequencies and modes, such as single sideband, which amateur radio operators commonly use. For optimum listening, a long wire can be attached to the standard antenna of any radio. Some radios have an accessory port where an extension antenna can be connected.

A learning curve must be negotiated if one hopes to become adept at shortwave listening (SWL). It's not as simple as turning your radio on. You must know what frequencies carry the information you need and when certain stations are on the air. That takes research and practice. Operating a radio is a diminishable skill. Over time, we tend to forget how to operate equipment. Wise preppers exercise survival skills regularly, and radio is no exception. If you want to be proficient in an emergency, practice using your radio at least once a month.

If you'd like to learn more about shortwave listening, check out the website swling.com. It has information about how to use a shortwave radio and program schedules.

19

Meshtastic

SOME OF THE TWO-WAY COMMUNICATION options described in this book require a license. For those who want a communication device that does not require a license, can be operated without internet or cellular service, and allows encrypted messaging, the Meshtastic app is worth considering.

The Meshtastic mobile app uses low power, long range (LoRa) radios. A radio is paired by Bluetooth with a phone or tablet. (We seldom think about the technology we use every day, but Bluetooth operates by sending and receiving radio signals. So do remote TV controllers and keyless car locks.) The Meshtastic app allows users to send encrypted text messages to anyone with a similar radio that is on the same frequency and within their radio's range. A channel is created on the app where users can invite others to join their channel, which allows them to send and receive messages to other channel members. In addition to messaging users in a channel, direct messages can be sent to individual users.

LoRa devices when used with the Meshtastic app create a *mesh network*. A mesh network is created when multiple devices communicate with each another over some distance. If two devices are connected at a distance of one mile, the range of the network is one mile. If a third device, or *node*, is connected at a distance of one mile, the range of the network becomes two miles. In this context, a node is a device that is connected to other devices by radio. As more nodes are added, the range of the network expands. With Meshtastic, a network of nodes is created that allows users to communicate by text message.

LoRa radios are little more than a printed circuit board with a processor, some software, a low power transmitter, an LCD screen, and a USB port. LoRa radios are inexpensive and can be purchased on eBay and other outlets. T-Beam and Rak are a couple of models sold presently. Some sellers offer radios that come in 3-D printed enclosures. A manufacturer I've purchased from has added a weatherproof enclosure and solar panel to one of his models.

In the U.S., LoRa radios operate on 915 MHz, which is designated for general public use. Thus, no license is required. In a suburban setting, the average range of a LoRa radio is a mile or two, depending on the elevation of the antenna, terrain, and obstacles that block the transmission of signals. However, I've tested two units outfitted with stock omnidirectional antennas placed 23 miles apart at elevations that allowed clear line of sight and successfully transmitted and received messages. (An omnidirectional antenna sends out a signal in all directions as opposed to a directional antenna, which transmits a signal in one direction.)

Using Meshtastic

To use Meshtastic, begin by attaching a suitable antenna to the LoRa radio. Most of the radios discussed in this book transmit when a button is pushed on a microphone or on the side of a handheld radio. LoRa radios do not have a transmit button or microphone. When powered on, they transmit automatically. Transmitting without an antenna can damage the radio. Do not power the radio on unless an antenna is attached. Most LoRa radios are powered by connecting them via a USB cable to a standard power outlet, a phone, solar battery bank, or another power source. Some newer models have built-in batteries and a power switch.

Once an antenna is attached, power on the radio. Open the Meshtastic app on your phone or tablet. Activate the Bluetooth feature on the mobile device and scan for a new device. Alternatively, in the app, you can go to the connection page (the farthest tab to the right—indicated with a gear icon) and connect to the radio by tapping on the plus (+) icon. During pairing, a numeric code will appear in large text on the LoRa radio's screen. Enter that number into your phone's PIN code verification window. Once the radio and phone are paired, you will see the radio ID displayed on the connection tab of the app. The ID is a series of numbers and letters that identifies the radio. The same ID will be displayed in small text on the radio's screen. You'll also see a cloud icon in the upper right corner of the app screen. A check mark will appear in the cloud icon to indicate that your device is paired. A diagonal line through the cloud icon means your phone or tablet is not paired. Lastly, a default device name will appear on the connection page. The device name can be changed if desired.

A default communication channel will be set up on the app. You can use it as is or modify it by changing the default settings. You'll find the page for modifying channels on the tab that is the second farthest from the right (indicated with a speaker icon). This page has five sections. In the top section, use the text box to give your channel a name. You can rename the existing channel, which essentially creates a new one. Note that the channel's name will contain a letter suffix (L, S, VL, etc). These letters indicate the data handling characteristics of the channel. The short option provides a shorter transmit and receive range but faster data throughput. Medium offers a slightly longer distance but slower data throughput. Long and very long increase range somewhat at the expense of data throughput.

The section below the text box displays a QR code that can be scanned by users you want to communicate with. The third section from the top creates a link that can be sent to them. The fourth section is for setting the parameters of the channel. You can choose from short to very long range and slow, medium, or fast sending speeds. A QR code scanning function is found at the bottom of the page. If someone invites you to their channel, scan the QR code on their app to be connected.

The tab that is second from the left (indicated by an icon with two people) displays the IDs of other radios within range. Tap on a device ID and a drop-down menu will appear that allows you to send the user a private message.

The tab farthest to the left (indicated by a chat icon) displays conversation threads—both messages on your channel and direct messages. Select a channel to begin a text chat with users who are connected to that channel. On this tab at the bottom of the page you'll find a text dialog box where you can compose and send messages.

With each message you attempt to send, a cloud icon will be visible next to the text box, indicating whether the text was sent. A check mark will appear in the cloud when a message is sent successfully. When it is not sent successfully, a diagonal line will appear through the cloud.

If you allow the Meshtastic app to provide notifications, you'll receive one when a new message is received. A handy feature with Meshtastic is the ability to save messages. Anytime a radio and phone are connected to another node, any received messages will be saved. You can check them at your convenience.

An invitation link can be sent to other users by text or email, or you can allow them to scan the QR code provided for your channel and acknowledge their request to join. All messages sent on the network are encrypted. Most LoRa radios feature GPS location, which can be turned off.

NOTE: The Bluetooth range for LoRa radios is about 25 feet. Keep your radio and phone close to one another so they will remain paired, which will keep the network operational. LoRa radios use very little current and frequently go into "sleep mode" to conserve power. If you try to send a message and there is a delay, it might be because the radio is in sleep mode. Most of these devices have a reset switch that can be used bring the radio out of sleep mode.

One way to deploy LoRa devices is to create a 4-device network that allows people in two distant homes to communicate with each other. Each home would deploy a weatherproof unit on the roof of their house to enable bidirectional transmission. A long-term power source would need to be supplied, as well as a phone or tablet positioned in an upper room or attic in range of each radio. (Any smartphone or tablet capable of loading the Meshtastic app can be used. It doesn't need to be connected to a cellular service and doesn't need a SIM card. It does need to be Bluetooth capable.) These two radios and mobile devices establish a network. Each home uses a second radio and mobile device to connect to their rooftop nodes. The rooftop nodes relay messages between users in the lower areas of the home, allowing them to send encrypted text messages via the mesh network. The range of this system depends on the height of the radio antennas and obstacles between the homes. If one location is 200 feet higher than the other and there is clear line of sight between the radios, the range can be 30 miles or more. In a typical suburban setting, the range might 2-3 miles or as much as 5-6 miles depending on terrain and obstacles.

There is an option to use the Meshtastic app as a licensed amateur radio operator. This enables the use of higher transmit power, but it turns off encryption. Take this into consideration before activating this option.

Low power UHF signals can easily be blocked. Successful long-range transmission relies on two radios having relatively clear line of sight. Signals may pass through a few trees but won't make it through a dense row of them. LoRa radios can be used for mobile operations, but effective deployment requires some planning. Using low power units requires the user to be in the ideal location.

In the 1970s, if you wanted to make a phone call and you were not at home, you had to find a phone booth. You could not make a phone call standing 100 feet north or south of a phone booth. You had to be inside the phone booth. Your exact location mattered. UHF radio transmission operates on a similar principle. You might not be able to transmit from the west edge of a parking lot, but a successful transmission might be sent from the east edge of the same parking lot. It's important to know where you are geographically in relation to the receiving unit and what obstacles are in the way. Position yourself in a location with the fewest obstructions between you and the receiving node.

20

Nextel Direct Talk

WHILE LoRa RADIOS AND THE Meshtastic app are a good grid-down option, the next device is a little easier to use, though it has limitations. Years ago, Nextel sold a phone with a low power UHF radio that transmits on half a watt of power. When not connected to the cell network, the phone's Direct Talk (not to be confused with Direct Connect) feature allows radio transmissions similar to the way a walkie-talkie works. Today, these radios are available used on eBay. They're prized by preppers who want a short-range communication device that works off-grid and doesn't require a license. Because the radio in these units is limited to less than 1 watt, it provides a coverage range of a mile or so, making it suitable for neighborhood or small team operations. The phones offer semi-secure talk groups.

The Direct Talk feature is available on more than a dozen models that were sold by Nextel years ago. Before purchasing one, make sure it offers the Direct Talk feature. Direct Talk does not require cell service, but it does require a SIM card to be inserted in the phone.

I'll provide instructions for operating the Nextel i365 model. (Other models will have a similar workflow for operation but will differ slightly.) To operate in Direct Talk mode, turn the phone on. When the "No Service" message appears, press the red phone button (end call). The phone will switch to "Direct

Talk" mode. You can now communicate with other phones (either as a group or individually) using the walkie-talkie feature. The walkie-talkie button is on the side of the phone.

The i365 phone has 10 channels and 15 privacy codes within each channel. Channels represent the radio frequencies on which you send and receive Direct Talk transmissions. Codes allow you to minimize interference from others using the same channel. To make Direct Talk Code calls, both parties must be on the same channel and code and have their phones set to Direct Talk. Be aware that others using both your same code and channel can hear your conversation, and you can hear theirs.

To set a channel and code:
1. In Direct Talk mode, press Edit (left softkey).
2. Select Channel.
3. Select a channel from the list.
4. Select Code
5. Select a code from the list.
6. Press Back (right softkey) to return to the Direct Talk standby screen.

To make a code call using Direct Talk, press and hold the push-to-talk button on the left side of the phone. The phone will display "Transmitting," along with the channel and code selected.

When you receive a code call using Direct Talk, your phone will display "Receiving," along with the channel and code selected. Answer a Direct Talk call by speaking wile pressing the push-to-talk button on the left side of the phone.

Private Direct Talk allows you to silence all the calls on a channel that are not directed specifically at you. To enable this feature, you must first set your phone to Private Only.

To set your phone to Private Only:
1. In Direct Talk mode, press Edit (left softkey).
2. Select Code.

3. Select Pvt Only.
4. Press Back (right softkey) to return to the Direct Talk standby screen. To reach you, other Direct Talk callers must be on your same channel and dial your ten-digit wireless phone number.

As with all UHF radios, transmission range is limited, but it can be improved by increasing your line of sight to the receiving station. If you're near a hill, try transmitting from the highest point on it. If a multi-story public building is nearby, consider going to the top floor. Does the building have an open balcony? If so, transmit from there. Off-grid communications require one to think outside the box.

21

Handheld Radios

SMALL RADIOS THAT CAN BE held in one hand are commonly referred to as walkie talkies or handy talkies. Amateur radio operators call them HTs. An HT is a compact radio powered by a removable, rechargeable battery. (If you anticipate using a handheld radio in a grid-down environment, consider buying a few spare batteries.) Handheld radios are generally sold with a short antenna that is referred to as a "rubber duck." This type of radio has a button that is depressed (usually located on the side of the radio) when the operator wants to transmit a message. HTs have built-in speakers for listening.

The typical handheld radio transmits a signal using less than 10 watts of power. The power limit for HTs is 10 watts, mainly due to restrictions imposed by batteries. The most common handheld radios transmit 5 watts of power. (Don't be surprised if you test your 5 watt handheld and find that it only transmits 4 watts.) A radio's power setting is an approximate gauge of how far a transmission can be heard by someone with a radio who is listening on the same frequency. A transmission using 1 watt of power will not be heard as far as a transmission using 5 watts of power when the same radio, antenna, and listening station are used. Using a stock antenna at ground level, the typical handheld radio might transmit a signal that can be received over a distance of three miles on 5 watts of power and one mile using 1 watt. It's worth repeating that the range of VHF and UHF radios is greatly affected by the presence of buildings, trees, and other objects that reflect and absorb radio waves. On flat ground, with no obstructions, VHF and UHF radio waves can be received over longer distances than in a dense forest or an urban location. The type of antenna used also affects the range over which a radio can transmit. (Antennas will be discussed in the next chapter.)

Advertising literature provided by radio manufacturers will often claim that a 5 watt radio can transmit up to 40 miles. A handheld radio can indeed transmit up to 40 miles or more, given the perfect circumstances. Line of sight transmission is enhanced when your position is elevated above ground level. If you stand atop a ten-story building, the horizon is not three miles away but 12 miles. If you stand on a mountaintop at an elevation of 3,000 feet, the horizon is more than 65 miles away. At this elevation, line of sight transmission is possible over great distances with a handheld radio because the horizon is further away. But most people don't operate in a perfect environment. Two operators using handheld radios with stock antennas at ground level in a suburban setting may be able to talk over a distance of a few miles.

Modes

Handheld radios can be used in a variety of modes. Direct transmission between two or more radios on a single frequency is referred to as *simplex* operation. Sometimes, stations will utilize two frequencies for communicating. Typically, an operator will transmit on one frequency while listening on another. This requires the user to monitor two frequencies—a capability that many radios have. This type of operation is referred to as *duplex* mode. In *half duplex,* only one operator talks at a time. When both stations can talk simultaneously without interference, it is referred to as *full duplex.*

If a third radio is used to relay transmissions between two stations, it is referred to as a *repeater* operation. A repeater, in the broadcast sense, is a radio that retransmits the signal of another radio. Some repeaters relay radio traffic on a single frequency. Some relay signals on two frequencies. A repeater, when elevated, can extend the range of a handheld radio for many miles. Repeaters that are available for public use are often located atop mountains, water towers, and tall buildings, which enhances line of sight. Amateur radio operators rely heavily on repeaters to extend the distance over which they can talk. But repeaters require power to work. In a crisis where power is not available, repeaters that you would normally rely on may not be operational. Some repeaters have battery, generator, or solar backup power, but many do not. For that reason, preppers should be familiar with simplex operation and incorporate into their plan other modes that do not rely on repeaters. (Other modes will be discussed in a later chapter.)

What Are Your Needs?

One of the most common questions people ask about radios is which one they should buy. If you're new to the world of portable radios, it's understandable that you would ask this question, but it can't be answered until other questions are answered first. Answering some basic questions will help narrow down the equipment and training you need.

- Are you interested primarily in listening to others who are on the air, or do you wish to talk via radio?

- If your goal is listening, buy a shortwave radio or scanner designed for listening rather than transmitting.

- With whom do you wish to communicate?

- Where are they located in relation to you geographically?

- Do you or the other party live on a hill or some other elevated location?

- Is there a mountain, hill, or other object that blocks the line of sight between you and the person with whom you wish to communicate?

- Is the other party willing to buy the needed equipment and learn how to use it?

- If those you wish to talk to are not willing to buy the equipment and learn how to use it, are you content to talk to strangers you might find who are on the air?

As we delve into the options available for radio communication, keep in mind the fact that you'll only be able to talk to someone if they have a radio tuned to the same frequency, operating in the same mode, and within range of your radio.

Citizen Band

Citizen Band (CB) radios have been designated by regulatory agencies for general public use in most countries. No license is required to operate them. In the U.S., 40 specific frequencies between 26.965 and 27.405 MHz have been allocated by the FCC for this band. These frequencies are also known collectively as channels 1-40. Citizen band radio transmission can be done in several modes: AM, FM, and single sideband. The maximum legal power limit is 4 watts on AM and FM, and 12 watts on single sideband. (Single sideband is a mode of transmission that decreases bandwidth without causing a reduction in power or signal strength.) Transmission of CB signals is usually by direct line of sight. The typical operating range is about 5 miles depending on terrain and obstructions. However, because the frequencies fall into the 11 meter HF spectrum, when atmospheric conditions are right, CB signals can travel by skywave for thousands of miles. (Skywave transmission will be discussed in depth in another chapter.) Handheld CB radios are available for purchase at truck stops and online retailers, as are units designed for use in a vehicle or as a base station at home.

FRS

If you want to talk to people within a few miles, a handheld radio may accomplish that goal without using a repeater. One option is a radio designated for use by the FCC under the Family Radio Service (FRS). These radios require no license. They operate in the UHF spectrum between 462-467 MHz. The effective range of FRS radio is about a mile and they are generally inexpensive. Their usefulness in prepping is limited to communication between people who are close in proximity to one another. FRS radios are very popular. In a situation where normal means of communication are not available, many people will be using them, and it may be hard to break through the chatter of other users. FRS radios can transmit on 22 channels. Some channels limit the power to half a watt. Other channels have a limit of 2 watts. FRS radios have preset power levels and the antennas cannot be changed.

MURS

Multi-use radio service (MURS) is a set of five frequencies designated by the FCC for public use. MURS frequencies are in the VHF spectrum between 151-154 MHz. MURS frequencies are not very popular, so if you're looking for an option where fewer ears are listening, and there's less traffic to compete with, MURS is worth looking into. MURS transmissions are limited to 2 watts maximum, which limits effective range. Radios dedicated to the MURS frequencies can be purchased through most retail outlets that sell radios. Some radios not designed explicitly for MURS will operate on MURS channels, though they may not be FCC-approved for MURS use.

If you want to talk to people who are more than a mile or two away, you'll need a different setup, which will necessitate a different radio, antenna, and possibly the use of a repeater.

Marine Band

In the U.S., the FCC has allocated a segment of the VHF spectrum for use by those who operate on waterways, although technically, anyone—regardless of their physical location—can use the marine band. The band includes frequencies between 156-174 MHz. Handheld radios are generally limited to 5 watts, while mobile units are limited to 25 watts. Mobile radios are designed to be used in vehicles, but they can also be used as a base station at your home. A 25 watt mobile radio with a good antenna can transmit 60 miles or more given the right conditions. The marine band is segmented into more than 80 channels. Some channels are restricted, while others are for general use. Be aware that if you use a 25 watt radio on a band that has a power limit of 2 watts, you should adjust the power level so that it complies with band's legal power limit.

GMRS

If you're not ready to make the jump to amateur radio, general mobile radio service (GMRS) is worth considering. Operating on GMRS frequencies in the U.S. requires an FCC license, but unlike with amateur radio, there is no test. One $35 license covers an entire family (and anyone else designated by the license holder). The license is good for ten years.

GMRS radios use the UHF spectrum between 462-467 MHz. Handheld radios generally offer 5 watts of power, while mobile units may operate on up to 50 watts, which could greatly extend the reach of your transmission if the frequency you're using permits it. GMRS repeaters are also available through retail outlets and can extend the range of handheld units. Some cities have GMRS repeaters that are available for public use without a fee. A search on the RepeaterBook website can help determine if there is a GMRS repeater near you.

The BTECH GMRS Pro radio has a unique feature. It pairs to a phone or tablet by Bluetooth, and when used with the BTECH mobile app, it allows text messages to be sent by GMRS radio. The transmitted messages are encoded as data packets and sent via radio frequency. The receiving party must be on the same frequency at the same time and within radio range, and they must have a device with the app installed to decode the message. For those who are accustomed to sending text messages, it's an option worth considering. It provides both convenience and a bit more security. The range of an off-the-shelf GMRS handheld radio and antenna is a few miles. With an improved antenna and repeater, it can be extended up to 100 miles.

Amateur Radio

Another option is to obtain an amateur (ham) radio license. The FCC licenses amateurs at three levels: technician, general, and extra. The technician is the lowest level. To obtain a technician license, you must pass a 35 question test and pay a $35 fee. Once you're licensed, you have the ability to operate on all VHF and UHF amateur bands and a small segment of the high frequency (HF) 10 meter band. The advantage of a ham license is that it gives you access to more radio bands and more repeaters. For example, there are dozens of amateur radio repeaters in the Phoenix area. Since most are located on mountaintops, I can use many of them, and some have emergency backup power.

Radio manufacturers must meet certain criteria for their radios to be accepted by the FCC for sale in the U.S. There is considerable controversy in the radio community over Chinese manufacturers and whether their units truly meet FCC requirements. And there is a faction within the amateur radio community that despises Chinese radio makers in general and Baofeng in particular. The radio hobbyist tends to prefer high-quality radios that are free of defects. They often look down on inferior models, particularly ones that operate outside of approved bands. If your interest is preparedness, you may not be concerned about minor performance issues or strict compliance with FCC regulations. The Baofeng UV-5R is the most popular handheld radio in the world, and for good reason. It's cheap. It's durable. It can be easily programmed, and it operates on bands its competitors don't. Because it's the most common radio in use today, chances are someone you know has one. Once you learn how to use the UV-5R, you can use the one someone else owns in a pinch without needing training.

Is It Approved?

The UV-5R can technically operate on all the bands mentioned above, including GMRS, MURS, marine, and the amateur 2 meter and 70 centimeter bands. I would like to note that although it is capable of operating on all these bands, the UV-5R is not approved by the FCC for use on all of them. It is approved for use on amateur 2 meter and 70 centimeter bands. Some variants are certified for operation on the amateur 1.25 meter band. The FCC has not approved the standard UV-5R for operation on MURS, GMRS and marine bands. If band compliance is a concern, Baofeng does make a UV-5R model that is FCC-approved for GMRS use. Despite this, I recommend that anyone who is interested in off-grid communications have at least one UV-5R, especially if you're new to the world of handheld radios. If you're looking for a first radio, it's a solid choice. Prepping involves teamwork, and a team of people can be outfitted with Baofeng radios for less than $100. If you have a little more money to spend, Yaesu, Icom, and Kenwood have entry-level radios that are worth considering.

Noise

There is always some degree of background noise present in the radio spectrum. Most HTs have a squelch function that allows the operator to filter out background noise. As the squelch is adjusted *upward*, more noise is filtered out. As the squelch is adjusted *downward*, more noise passes through the filter and is heard by the operator. A word of caution is warranted here: Although the squelch function filters out noise, it also filters out radio transmissions without distinction except to signal strength. If you think setting your radio's squelch on the highest setting will keep you from hearing noise, it will certainly do that. But it will also prevent you from hearing weak but readable signals from people with whom you may want to communicate. For general use, set your squelch to the lowest setting that filters out background noise but allows weak signals to be heard.

A radio transmission is heard when the transmitted signal is stronger than the background noise. When a transmitted signal can be heard, it is said to be "above the noise floor." The most common type of radio signal is analog. Analog signals vary in strength, sometimes breaking above the noise floor and other times being below it. When this happens, the message is only partly heard. The part that is heard is that which breaks above the noise floor.

Signal to Noise

A comparison of the strength of a radio signal to the noise that is present is called signal-to-noise ratio (SNR). The goal of radio operations is sending and receiving signals that are stronger than the ambient noise. Measures taken to boost a radio signal will help that endeavor, as will steps taken to reduce the noise. Most electronic devices, like computers, printers, televisions, etc., emit noise that interferes with radio signals. Many of these devices have a ferrite bead attached to the power cord to suppress noise, but some do not. A ferrite bead is a cylindrical device attached to a power cord or antenna cable that dissipates noise. If you hear excessive noise on your radio, check to see if a nearby electronic device has a ferrite bead on its power cord. If it does not, consider purchasing one and installing it. The core in a ferrite bead is made from a mix of different powdered metals—mostly iron. The combination is called the "mix." There are different mixes for different frequencies. The mix used for the ham radio spectrum is called mix31 and helps eliminate noise on bands between 160 meters and 70 centimeters.

Some radios are equipped with internal noise filters, but they work with mixed results. The one I've used successfully is a bandwidth filter. By narrowing the received bandwidth, you can sometimes remove enough noise to hear a transmission that is otherwise unreadable. I've also used a device called a current choke balun on my HF radio to filter out stray electrical signals. Another option is to simply move your antenna away from a known source of interference. Generally speaking, the higher an antenna is located above ground, the better it will send and receive signals. But that is true of all signals, including unwanted noise. If you experience excessive noise, you might try lowering the height of your antenna. Many antennas designed purely for listening are set up on the ground or just a few feet above it. While such an arrangement drastically reduces the received signal, it reduces the noise much more and often yields an excellent signal-to-noise ratio. In a later chapter, we'll discuss the tactical use of low height antennas.

Analog Versus Digital

Most handheld radios transmit an analog FM signal. An analog FM signal uses a wide segment of the radio spectrum. Analog signals have variations in signal quality that can make it difficult to understand a message. Some radios have the option of transmitting a digital signal in addition to analog ones. While analog signals vary in strength relative to the noise floor, digital signals do not operate this way. A digital signal is uniform in strength. Radios capable of receiving them capture either the entire signal or none of it. When a digital message is transmitted, the receiving station will either receive the entire message or no message at all. Digital signals are more efficient than analog ones. A digital signal uses less bandwidth compared to an analog one, providing a bit more punch for a transmission at a given power setting.

Analog radios cannot receive digital signals. Thus, digital signals are less susceptible to eavesdropping. The technology used to build a digital transmitter is more expensive than its analog counterpart, thus digital capable radios cost more than analog ones. Yaesu, Icom, Kenwood, and other manufacturers make radios capable of transmitting and receiving digital signals. Some models are digital only. Some offer both analog and digital and most of these models feature automatic detection of analog and digital modes. These radios switch automatically to either analog or digital mode depending on the type of signal that is received.

22

VHF and UHF Antennas

THE TWO BIGGEST PROBLEMS FOR users of handheld radios are the limited range offered by stock antennas and line of sight transmission. These limitations are generally overcome in one of two ways. If you can increase the height of your antenna, you extend the horizon and increase your effective range. The other option is to boost the radio signal so it can be heard more clearly. In this chapter, we'll look at ways to increase signal strength through better antenna design and placement.

Handheld radios are sold with a stock antenna, but not all antennas are created equal. For example, although the Baofeng UV-5R is a good radio, the stock antenna provided with it is not tuned to the frequencies the radio operates on. To maximize the power of a radio, the antenna must be tuned to the operating frequency. When it is not, the power that should be converted to an electromagnetic wave is converted to heat, which can damage the radio. You won't damage a handheld radio by using the stock antenna from the manufacturer, but if it is not well tuned to the band you're using, your signal will not travel as far. Not all stock antennas are poorly tuned. My Yaesu handheld radio came with a stock antenna that is tuned perfectly for the amateur bands that I use. The only way to know if your antenna is tuned to the bands you want to use is to test it, which we will discuss next.

SWR

When we evaluate the efficiency of an antenna, we're comparing the amount of power that goes forward through the antenna with the amount of power that is reflected back toward the radio. The comparison of forward power to reflected power is expressed as the standing wave ratio (SWR). The perfect standing wave ratio is 1:1, which indicates that 100 percent of the power is being transmitted forward, with none of it being reflected back toward the radio. When 5 watts of power is transmitted by the radio, the antenna sends all 5 watts into the atmosphere. If the SWR of an antenna is less than 2:1 on the operating frequency, the antenna will perform well. Once the SWR rises above 3:1, efficiency drops off, and the antenna is less usable.

Measuring SWR

I wanted to know how well my HT antennas were tuned, so I purchased a device that measures SWR. The Surecom SW 102 is easy to use and reliable for this type of work. The test involves connecting an adapter to the radio and another adapter to the antenna. The radio is turned on, the push to talk button is pressed and a signal is transmitted. The SWR and power output are displayed. I routinely perform this test on all the antennas I use with any radio. If the SWR is excessively high on the bands I commonly use, I find a better antenna.

I prefer Nagoya antennas as a replacement for the stock antenna that comes with the Baofeng UV-5R. (Be aware that popular antennas by companies like Nagoya are copied and sold as if they are genuine. Performance of knock-offs are unpredictable.) Even though it is marketed as a GMRS antenna, the Nagoya NA 771G is well-tuned for the 70 centimeter and 2 meter amateur bands as well as GMRS. **TIP:** If you replace a stock antenna, be sure that the replacement has a connector that is compatible with your radio.

The Surecom SW 102 provides a snapshot of the efficiency of an antenna on a single frequency. The Nano VNA can provide a look at SWR across multiple bands at once. I recommend getting one, especially if you intend to build your own antennas, which I also recommend for many practical reasons that will be discussed shortly.

Resonant Antennas

Several factors affect the efficiency of an antenna, but none make a greater impact than the length of the antenna wire, which is sometimes called the antenna *element*. An antenna element is little more than a wire cut to a certain length that is connected to a radio. When the wire is the same length as the radio wave being transmitted, the wire is said to be *resonant*. A length of wire two meters long is resonant on the 2 meter radio frequency. This wire can be called a full wave resonant element since its length is two meters—the same as the wavelength with which it is used. A wire that is one meter in length would be called a half-wave resonant element for the 2 meter band. Even though this wire is not the length of a full wave, it will transmit a signal with high efficiency on that frequency. A wire that is half a meter in length would be called a quarter wave element for the 2 meter band because it is a quarter of the length of a two meter wave. Most two meter HT antennas are constructed to be a quarter wave in length, or approximately 19 inches. However, you'll find that most 2 meter HT antennas are not 19 inches long. The physical length of an antenna can be shortened by coiling part of the element wire. This produces an element that is electrically a quarter wave long but an antenna that is physically shorter.

A vertical wire used as an antenna radiates an electromagnetic wave that travels equally in all directions and is called an *omni-directional* antenna. This type of antenna sends a small portion of the total signal in all directions. This arrangement has one major advantage and one drawback. The advantage is that anyone within range who is listening can receive the signal. The drawback is that anyone who does receive it is getting a weak signal that may not be above the noise floor. Thus, the message may not be readable. Is there a way to boost the signal to make it stronger? Yes, there is.

Yagi Antennas

The Yagi antenna is designed to increase the strength (gain) of a radio signal. When a signal's strength is boosted, it rises above the noise floor, making it more readable. A Yagi is a directional antenna, meaning it sends and receives radio signals in a specific direction. It is composed of a single long beam with several elements attached at a 90 degree angle to the beam. The Yagi antenna is connected to a radio with a length of coaxial cable and pointed in the direction the operator wishes to transmit and receive. I regularly used a Yagi with a handheld radio to talk to a friend who lives ten miles away. I've done testing in an elevated location with good line of sight and transmitted to another operator 20 miles away who was using an HT with a stock antenna.

A Yagi antenna is a game-changer for anyone who wants to communicate over long distances with a handheld radio. The main drawback is that since it is a directional antenna, you need to know the direction of the person (or repeater) you want to communicate with. If you don't know where the intended listener is located, a Yagi may not be the ideal antenna, but you could transmit in a few directions and see if the other party answers.

Yagi antennas come in different configurations, mostly having to do with the number of elements. A three element Yagi has a main shaft with three cross members (elements). A five element Yagi has five cross members. The more cross members that are added, the more the signal is boosted. But keep in mind that the more elements that are added, the more directional the antenna becomes. A three element Yagi is only slightly directional, meaning that if the person you want to talk to is located north of you and you point the antenna west, you can still make contact. But aiming the antenna south would prevent them from receiving the transmission. Using a five element Yagi, if your target is north and you pointed the antenna west, you may not make contact. With a seven element Yagi, precise aiming becomes critical because it is a highly directional antenna.

Because the Yagi boosts signal strength, you can operate on lower power and still make contact with others. A mantra of ham radio is to use the lowest power necessary to make contact. This is particularly important in a grid-down situation where radios are operated on batteries that must be charged in a way other than household current. Most HTs allow the user to select from several power settings. Working on low power conserves battery life. Another feature of the Yagi is its ability to conceal your location. In a hostile environment, where an opponent may be trying to locate you by direction finding, a lower power radio connected to a Yagi puts out a small electronic signature that is hard to detect, whereas an omni-directional antenna on a 5 watt radio is more easily detected.

I usually hold my Yagi antenna in my hand and aim it in the direction of a repeater I want to use or the person I want to talk to. (The Yagi I use has a foam grip on the end of the main beam, which makes it easy to hold with one hand.) I hold the antenna with cross members in an up and down (vertical) direction. Generally, FM antennas are used with the elements in a verti-cal position, while modes like single sideband use a horizontal orientation. Both sending and receiving stations should use the same antenna orientation for UHF and VHF.

Holding an antenna with one hand and a radio with the other can be problematic. One solution is to secure your radio to your body with a belt clip or harness made to hold it. A lapel speak-er-microphone will allow you to transmit without needing to hold the radio to your mouth. Voice-activated headsets are another option.

A Yagi antenna can be mounted on a pole for permanent or semi-permanent installation. It's not difficult to mount one to the eave of your house. If you position it out of view from the street, it may not be noticed by neighbors or your HOA. Plac-ing your antenna in an elevated location enhances line of sight transmission by extending the horizon. A permanently mounted antenna requires a coaxial cable to connect it to a radio. Coaxial cable can be installed on the exterior of a house and painted to match the trim and can be concealed inside painted PVC pipe to look like conduit if necessary.

NOTE: Amateur radios (with a couple of exceptions) use 50 ohm coaxial cable. Do not use 75 ohm cable, which is designed for other applications. For radio operations with a handheld Yagi, I recommend RG-316 cable with connectors to match your equipment. For permanent or semi-permanent installation, consider RG-8, RG-8X, KMR-400, or LMR-400 cable.

If you want to build your own Yagi antenna, you can find plans online. Many companies make them commercially. I recommend Arrow's line of Yagi antennas if you prefer a professionally made model. When building or purchasing a Yagi, keep in mind that the GMRS frequencies of 462-467 megahertz are close to the UHF 70 centimeter ham frequencies of 420-450 megahertz. A single Yagi, if it is tuned correctly, can operate well on all these frequencies. Yagi antennas that are commercially made usually have a way of tuning the antenna to the desired frequency. Lastly, consider the fact that accessory antennas may not have the same type of connector as your radio. Since a length of coaxial cable is required to connect an HT to a Yagi, be sure to get a cable with connectors that match the antenna and the radio with which it is to be used.

23

HF Radio

LONG BEFORE THE INTERNET WAS invented, people communicated with friends and strangers around the world through the amateur high frequency (HF) radio bands. HF radio was the first internet, and it may well be the next one.

The drawback of VHF and UHF radio is that (with a few exceptions) transmissions are limited to line of sight. There is some blurring in the VHF radio spectrum with respect to how signals travel. In the higher VHF frequencies, waves travel exclusively by line of sight. But as one moves into the lower frequencies, occasionally, waves travel by skipping off the ionosphere in what is called *skywave propagation*. The VHF spectrum between 50-54 megahertz, known as the 6 meter band, behaves the same way the lower frequency HF bands do. Signals are transmitted primarily by skywave. This chapter deals exclusively with radio bands that use skywave propagation.

Skywave propagation describes a radio wave that is transmitted through the lower atmosphere into the higher ionosphere, where it collides with ionized particles. When the ionosphere is sufficiently charged by electromagnetic energy from the sun, the radio wave is reflected back to Earth, where other radio operators receive it. That is skywave propagation. Because HF radio waves skip off the ionosphere, they can travel thousands of miles, making international communication possible.

Although it is important for UHF and VHF antennas to be deployed in the same direction (vertically or horizontally), it is not an issue when using HF radios. Vertical and horizontal signals are scrambled in the ionosphere, making it possible to receive signals from a vertical antenna on a horizontal one and vice versa.

Licensing

If you live in the U.S., the right to transmit via HF radio requires a license from the FCC. (No license is required for listening.) The technician license allows one to dip their toes into the world of HF with privileges on a small part of the 10 meter band. The general license holder has access to all the HF bands but not the entirety of all bands. That privilege is reserved for the extra class license holder. If you happen to be an electrical engineer, you might be able to pass the technician test with a bit of studying. But if you're a retired paramedic who knows little about electronics and physics, you'll need to study for a few weeks to pass the test. The general test is more difficult than the technician but is doable with a week or two of additional study. Many people take practice tests for a couple of weeks before taking the license test. Practice tests present you with questions taken from the actual pool of questions you'll see on the license test. With repetition, you can memorize the correct answers. Practice tests for amateur licenses are available on many websites and mobile apps.

I believe HF radio will become an essential communication service in the future, though at present, it is mostly thought of as an obscure hobby. If we experience a widespread, prolonged power outage or a sustained disruption of the internet, HF radio will likely become the main method by which people communicate nationally and internationally. While telecom companies control cellular services and the internet, control of amateur radio is in the hands of millions of independent operators around the globe. It is the preeminent decentralized global communication platform.

HF radio is capable of transmitting voice communications, text messages, image files, and much more. One of the earliest uses of radio was sending messages by Morse code, which is still popular today. It may sound like an archaic practice, but the dots and dashes of Morse code use RF signals very efficiently. When atmospheric conditions don't allow voice communication, Morse code often gets through, and on less power. Morse code is sent by connecting to a radio a device called a keyer, which can be purchased for as little as $10.

Space Weather

UHF and most VHF signals are not dependent on atmospheric conditions. These signals can be sent and received without consideration of weather. That is not true of HF radio, which requires certain ionospheric conditions to be present. Weather conditions that impact HF radio can be broadly lumped into two categories. Some atmospheric changes occur daily and can be accounted for in a communications plan. Others arise spontaneously and can't easily be anticipated in advance.

The ionosphere is the uppermost level of the atmosphere. Its lowest layer begins about 40 miles above sea level and can extend up to 600 miles in height. It has three layers that are referred to as the D, E, and F layers. The D layer is the lowest layer (closest to the Earth). The E layer lies above it, with the F layer being uppermost (farthest from the Earth).

Every day at dawn, the D layer of the ionosphere begins to receive radiation from the rising sun. As it does, two things happen simultaneously. Low frequency radio waves are being absorbed in the D layer, while waves that are higher in frequency are reflected back to Earth. Specifically, radio waves below a frequency of around 7 MHz are blocked during the day, while those that are above 7 MHz bounce off the D layer and return to Earth where they can be heard by listening stations. At night, when the sun no longer provides ionizing radiation, the D layer disappears. The E and F layers combine into one layer, which reflects low frequency radio waves back to Earth. This sets up a predictable pattern where low frequency signals are sent and received more reliably in the evening, and higher frequency signals are more easily sent and heard during daylight hours. That covers the predictable changes HF operators must consider. Now, let's discuss factors that are less predictable.

The transmission of HF signals is enhanced by increased sunspot activity. Sunspots are dark regions of strong magnetic fields on the surface of the sun. They appear darker because they are cooler than their surroundings. Sunspots energize the ionosphere, allowing HF radio waves to reflect back to the Earth more reliably. In general, the more sunspots there are on a given day, the better conditions will be for HF operators. Although it is not possible to predict how many sunspots will be present on a given day, we can track the general trend.

The sun goes through an 11-year solar cycle where sunspot activity as a whole increases and decreases. The point in the cycle where sunspot activity is lowest is called the solar minimum. HF radio transmission is most challenging during this time. The point in the solar cycle where sunspot activity is highest is called the solar maximum. Conditions for HF transmissions are favorable during the solar maximum. As this book goes to print late in 2023, we are moving toward a solar maximum that should peak in 2025. Atmospheric conditions have been favorable this year, with many operators using the 28 megahertz (10 meter) band—a frequency that has been unusable for years due to inadequate sunspot activity.

Lastly, we must consider solar storms. The sun is prone to flinging waves of electromagnetic radiation into space in the form of solar flares and coronal mass ejections. These phenomena, when directed at Earth, interfere with radio transmissions. Solar storms can be predicted a few days in advance, and there are websites that provide space weather forecasts. But a radio operator without access to the internet doesn't know from one day to the next if a magnetic storm will interfere with their plans. It's not difficult however, to know if a solar storm is active. If you tune your radio to a band that is usually busy with radio traffic and all you hear is noise, there's a good chance a solar storm is blocking signal transmission. Fortunately, solar storms are short, lasting anywhere from a few hours to a couple of days. Once the storm has passed, conditions will return to normal.

In summary, HF radio has both predictable patterns for use and occasional unplanned disruptions. Because it allows communication around the globe, it is useful when internet and cell phone services are not available.

As I mentioned, lower HF frequencies are best used at night, while higher frequencies are better during the day. Specifically, the 40 meter (7 MHz), 60 meter (5 MHz), 80 meter (3.5 MHz), and 160 meter (1.8 MHz) bands are more usable at night. In contrast, the 30 meter (10 MHz) 20 meter (14 MHz), 17 meter (18 MHz), 15 meter (21 MHz), 12 meter (24 MHz), and 10 meter (29 MHz) bands are best used during daylight hours. This is a general guideline only and not a hard and fast rule. Some of the higher frequencies can be used at night, and some of the lower frequencies are usable during the day. The 40, 30, and 20 meter bands are often usable 24 hours a day.

Which Radio?

As for equipment, I'll make some suggestions, but before making a purchase, you might contact your local amateur radio club and ask if any members have equipment you can use. I know a couple of people who contacted their local clubs and were gifted some very nice equipment by hams who wanted to encourage them. Experienced hams are called *Elmers,* and thousands of them are willing to help new hams get up the learning curve.

Once you're licensed, you should start acquiring the gear needed to get on the air, although some people buy their equipment first. After all, no license is required to listen. New HF radios start at around $500. Some of the more expensive models cost $20,000.

The Yaesu FT-817 and FT-818 are not available for purchase new, but used models can be found on eBay for around $400, depending on condition. There is little difference between the two models. They're time-tested units that offer a lot of features in a small package. They operate on all amateur HF, VHF, and UHF bands in multiple modes. Two antenna connectors are available, along with an internal battery, which is rare. Most HF radios require an external 12-volt power supply, but the 817 comes with a wall outlet adapter and an internal battery. (Some users complain about the weak battery supplied with the 817, but an aftermarket lithium battery is available.) The weakness of the 817 is that it's only capable of transmitting on 5 watts. However, an aftermarket 45 watt amplifier is available for this model if you need more power. The 817 can be used as a base unit, but its lightweight and small size make it an excellent choice for portable operations.

Another option is the pocket-sized FX-4CR, which sells for $550. It operates on all amateur bands between 80 and 6 meters. The maximum power output is 20 watts—a respectable figure for a small radio. It has a built-in sound card, which is helpful for digital modes, and a screen that displays the radio spectrum in what is known as a *waterfall*. A waterfall display lets you see signals on a spectrum without having to tune to a frequency to find out if the frequency is being used. A quick glance at the waterfall will tell you where the traffic is on a given band. The FX-4CR comes with a power cord and compact microphone. It can be powered by several off-grid options, including a battery or 12-volt cigarette lighter with a suitable adapter. Its machined aluminum case measures 4 inches wide, 2.5 inches deep, and 1.75 inches high. It weighs one pound, making it ideal for portable operations.

If you're willing to spend around $1,000, you might consider either the Icom 7300 or the Yaesu FT-991A. These radios can operate on all modes and all bands. Radios in this class generally transmit a maximum of 100 watts of power. They offer touchscreen menus and waterfall displays. They're generally used as base units, as their weight makes them less suitable for portable operations. There are many other good radios in this class that you might consider. Be aware that HF radios are often in high demand and may not be available for months at a time. Also, be advised that some of the more popular radios for sale on eBay are not manufactured for use in the United States, but in Japan. Before buying a radio on eBay, ask the seller to confirm that it's a U.S. version if you live in the United States.

24

HF Antennas

BECAUSE THEIR WAVELENGTHS ARE SHORT, UHF and VHF radios can use compact antennas. A half-wave antenna for the 40 meter HF band is 20 meters (66 feet) in length. How does one position a 66-foot-long wire to be used as an antenna? While HTs have short antennas that screw into a port on top of the radio, HF antennas are generally mounted to a structure and connected to a radio using a length of cable called a *feed line*. A variety of feed line types are used with HF radios. We'll discuss some of the more common ones, but let's begin with a discussion of antenna design.

You can have a great radio, but if your antenna is designed or built poorly, you won't transmit or receive signals very well. You should put at least as much thought into choosing or building your antenna as buying your radio. Consider the fact that each radio band you use requires an antenna tuned to that frequency.

One option is the multi-band antenna—a single antenna that allows operation on multiple bands. Multi-band antennas offer great flexibility. Many hams build their own multi-band antennas, but some prefer to purchase commercially made ones. Prices run the gamut from cheap to expensive, depending on construction type and how many bands are offered. The limiting factor for most people is space. As mentioned, HF antennas are not generally compact. They require either vertical or horizontal real estate, and that must be considered before buying or building an antenna. A second issue is cost. Well-made antennas cost hundreds and sometimes thousands of dollars.

Some hams prefer a commercially made vertical antenna. These antennas are usually secured to a tower or another stationary object. An ideal location is a rooftop, but most HOAs forbid mounting an antenna on the roof. Many people don't have the space required for a long wire antenna or the ability to erect a permanent tower. For every problem, there is a solution if you're willing to think outside the box. Many people deploy HF antennas in their attics. It's not the ideal setup, but it works. For apartment dwellers and others who have minimal space, consider using a loop antenna, which is compact enough to fit into a small space.

80 Meter Antenna

A popular HF antenna is an 80 meter end-fed, half-wave dipole. It's made from a wire approximately 130 feet long (half the length of an 80 meter wave). It's called a *dipole* because it has two elements that transmit the radio wave. One element is the 130 foot wire. The second element is a shorter wire that will be discussed shortly. It is called an end-fed because a feed line is connected to one end of the wire, while the other end is secured to a stationary object.

Wire antennas can be mounted either horizontally or vertically. Some people deploy them in a vee configuration. Equally popular is the inverted vee, where the center is higher than the ends. Sometimes the radiating element is suspended horizontally between two stationary objects (see illustration). It may be deployed at a sloping angle with one end near the ground and the other end at considerable height. Each configuration has benefits and drawbacks with respect to performance. A bonus of the 80 meter end-fed is that it will operate on most of the bands between 6 and 80 meters without needing a tuner. The 40 meter version of the end-fed dipole is 66 feet long and is usable on the 40, 20, 15, and 10 meter bands without needing a tuner.

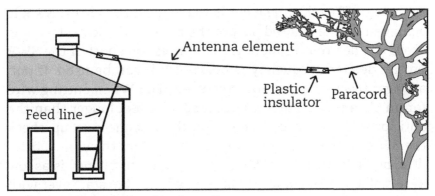

HF dipole antenna deployed horizontally

Tuning

A long wire antenna can be used for listening to radio signals without worrying about its precise length. But if it is to be used for transmitting a signal, the exact length is important. For signal transmission, wire antennas must be cut to the proper length so they resonate on a particular band or frequency. *Tuning* an antenna is adjusting the length of the elements so they resonate on the desired band or frequency. I'll explain how to tune the 80 meter antenna I just described. (This is where a Nano VNA or similar device comes in handy.)

Using a device capable of measuring SWR, connect it to the feed point of the antenna using an adapter if necessary. Measure the SWR on the 80 meter (3.5 MHz) band. Here's how to do it: The antenna should be deployed as it would be in normal use. The SWR meter is set to measure the SWR across the 80 meter band. The SWR is displayed as a horizontal line with peaks and valleys. Peaks in the line indicate frequencies where the SWR is high. Dips indicate frequencies where the SWR is low. The goal is to adjust the length of the radiating element so that the SWR is below 2:1 on the frequency you intend to use. (The closer to 1:1 the better.) If the lowest point of the SWR dip is *below* the frequency to be used, the wire is too long and should be cut a few inches shorter. As the wire is shortened, the lowest point on the SWR dip should move higher in frequency. The SWR is re-measured each time a cut is made until the lowest SWR is achieved on the desired part of the band. If the lowest SWR is *above* the desired frequency, the wire is too short. If the SWR on the desired frequency is below 2:1, it can be used. If not, a longer piece of wire should be used. **TIP:** When cutting wire for an HF antenna, always cut it several feet longer than the anticipated length you'll need. After the antenna is set up, check the SWR on the band you intend to use. Trim the wire shorter little by little until the SWR on the desired frequency is as low as possible. If you cut it too short, you'll need to start over with a new wire.

Impedance

An end-fed antenna—a wire with the feed point at the end—generates high impedance. Impedance is the opposition to electrical flow, measured in ohms. In many cases, an antenna and its feed line will have disproportionate impedance values. The coaxial cable typically used to connect an antenna and an amateur radio has 50 ohms of impedance. An end-fed dipole will generate between 1,800-5,000 ohms of impedance, depending on how it is deployed. For safety and efficiency, impedance mismatches must be resolved. This is done by connecting a transformer between the antenna and the feed line. A transformer reduces the impedance of the radiating element. A 36:1 or 49:1 transformer will help match the impedance of very long wires. A 4:1 or 9:1 transformer can be used with shorter wires.

Transformers come in two types. A *balun* is used to connect a balanced line to an unbalanced line. (The word bal-un signifies the relationship of **bal**anced-to-**un**balanced.) An *unun* connects an unbalanced line to an unbalanced line. (The name un-un signifies the relationship of **un**balanced-to-**un**balanced.) A balanced line is one where both elements have the same impedance. An unbalanced line is one where the impedance is different and must be changed.

Transformers usually have two connecting posts. The wire that is to be the radiating element is connected to one post, which may have an antenna symbol. The second wire is connected to the other post, which is typically labeled with a ground symbol. The second wire is usually a few meters in length, depending on the frequency to be used. This wire is called a *counterpoise*.

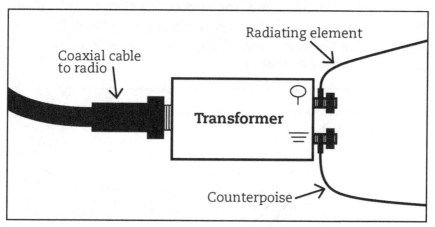

Transformer connected to antenna wires and feed line

Since it is not convenient to anchor a long wire in a vertical position, HF antennas are often deployed horizontally. Typically, one end is secured to an insulated metal pole, chimney or some other structure near the home, and the other end is secured to a tree using plastic insulators. An antenna placed in a horizontal orientation sends some of the RF energy toward the sky and some toward the ground. Strictly speaking, this arrangement will work, though it could be better. The RF that is directed toward the ground is wasted unless a device is used to re-direct some of it skyward. A *ground plane* is one such device.

Counterpoise

For horizontal antennas, a counterpoise is used to create a ground plane. A counterpoise is (generally) a length of wire that runs parallel to the ground. It provides a ground plane that reflects some of the radio waves back toward the sky, which increases signal strength. Most end-fed dipoles require a transformer to be placed between the radiating element and the feed line that goes to the radio. Most transformers are built with a post that is used to attach a counterpoise wire. The counterpoise wire is secured to that post and runs above or along the ground away from the feed point. The ideal length of a counterpoise wire is five percent of the lowest wavelength to be used. The 80 meter frequency has a wavelength of 262 feet. Five percent of 262 is roughly 13 feet. A counterpoise for 40 meters will be approximately 7.5 feet long.

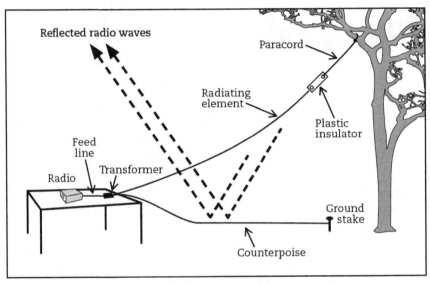

Typical deployment of an HF dipole antenna with counterpoise

Depending on how you connect your antenna to your radio, you may not need a counterpoise. If your antenna has a feed line longer than 15 feet, the feed line itself may act as a counterpoise. The transformer manufacturer will be able to provide guidance as to whether you need a counterpoise or not.

Radials

Vertical antennas generally use radials to create a ground plane. Commercially made UHF and VHF antennas typically have three or four short wires protruding horizontally from the base. These are the radials that create a ground plane. Vertical HF antennas usually require several wires to be connected to the base and positioned on the ground in a pattern that radiates outward from the center. If you purchase a commercially made vertical antenna, the manufacturer can provide guidance as to the number and length of wires needed. Typically, at least four are required, with each wire being a quarter wave in length. Eight to ten wires will provide a stronger signal. Efficiency tends to peak at 16 wires. The radials do not need to be placed in a perfect circular pattern. Whatever arrangement your property allows is fine. Radials do not need to be the same length. If multiple bands are used, some should be shorter and some longer.

Random Wire

Another option is to build a non-resonant wire antenna. The *random wire* antenna is not cut to resonate on a particular frequency. Instead, it's cut to a length that allows it to operate with acceptable SWRs on multiple bands. As an example, when used with a suitable transformer, a wire approximately 135 feet in length will give SWRs below 1.8:1 on all HF bands between 160 and 6 meters. (The actual length of such an antenna will vary depending on the thickness of the wire used.) According to several companies that sell antenna transformers, a 74-foot-long wire will yield good results on bands between 80 and 10 meters. A 36-foot-long wire will give usable SWRs on bands between 10 and 40 meters. The best approach to building a random wire antenna is to determine how much space you have available, which will determine the maximum length of wire you can use. Longer wires will allow you to operate on lower frequencies.

Tuners

An antenna may be resonant on the frequency you want to use, but sometimes, the SWR will be high on part of a particular band. If your radio has an internal tuner, you can use it to improve the SWR on the frequency you intend to use. Bear in mind that tuners have limitations, and they will not tune on a frequency that has an excessively high SWR. The limit is typically 3:1. The best approach is to cut an antenna wire to the length that provides the lowest SWR on the desired band. When a multiband antenna is used, the wire is cut to give the lowest SWR on as many bands as possible, and the tuner is used to fine-tune each frequency. An external tuner is used in the same way.

Station Grounding

HF radios, tuners, and amplifiers operate on voltages that can be dangerous. Many of these devices have ground lugs located somewhere on the chassis. Here's one way to ground radios, tuners, amplifiers, and other equipment: Purchase a grounding bus bar that has enough terminal connectors for each piece of equipment you need to ground. Mount it somewhere near your equipment. My gear sits atop a portable workbench. I zip-tied a bus bar to one of the legs of the bench, and cut lengths of wire long enough to reach from each piece of equipment to the bus bar. For grounding, stranded wire is not advised; 10 gauge solid copper THHN is better. Crimp suitable connectors to the ends of each wire and connect one to each piece of equipment to be grounded. Connect the other end of each wire to a terminal on the bus bar.

The Window Pass Through

One headache for ham radio operators is making a way for cables and wires to safely enter and exit the home. MFJ makes a line of cedar window pass-through devices that have connectors for 50 ohm feed line, long wire antennas, and grounding stubs. The pass-through is a cedar board with a metal insert that encases various adapters. It is cut to length and sits in a window opening. It comes with a strip of foam insulation attached but it's not high quality. I recommend removing and replacing it with commercially made weather stripping. Once cut to length, it can be painted to match your house, if desired. When it has been prepared, place it in an opening, and close the window. The standard window latch will not be usable, but an anti-burglar bar can be used to prevent the window from being opened from outside. Cut a piece of grounding wire long enough to reach from the bus bar to the ground stub on the window pass-through. Connect one end of it to the bus bar. Now, hammer a copper grounding stake into the ground near the window. Be sure to check first that you're not going to hit plumbing, internet, power, or other utility lines or pipes. Cut a length of wire that reaches from the outside stub of the window pass-through to the ground stake. Attach a ring terminal to the end that will be connected to the ground stub on the window-pass through. Connect the other end to the ground stake using a mechanical connection. (Do not solder this connection.) Whenever possible, the ground rod for your radios should be bonded to your home's electrical service panel ground. You now have a properly grounded station and a way to connect outdoor antennas to your radio. I also advise connecting a lightning arrester to the feed line of an outdoor antenna at the point where it enters your home. Lightning arrestors have a terminal that must be connected to a ground stake using a mechanical (non-soldered) connection as the high voltage of a lightning bolt can destroy soldered connections.

How High?

An antenna used for skywave propagation should be deployed at a height somewhere between one-half and one-quarter of a wavelength of the desired frequency above ground. This height allows radio waves to achieve the best takeoff angle, which optimizes their ability to skip off the ionosphere. An 80 meter antenna should be positioned (at the highest point) somewhere between 20 and 40 meters (66-130 feet) above ground. For this reason, some ham radio operators erect towers for their antennas. But for many people, ham radio is a game of compromise. Lot size, lack of trees, finances, HOA restrictions, and plain old practicality require many of us to come up with a less-than-ideal plan that works. The 80 meter dipole antenna described above can be used at a height of 15 feet above ground. It won't be as efficient as one deployed at the ideal height, but it will work, and it provides an interesting benefit, which will be examined in another chapter.

Single Band

Although multi-band antennas are nice, they are optional. If you're content to operate on a single radio band with an antenna dedicated to that band, you might consider the 20 meter band. It's a popular band worldwide, and it's usable during the day and night. The wire for an end-fed half-wave dipole for the 20 meter band is approximately 33 feet long. It can be constructed with a couple of lengths of wire and a 4:1 transformer. While lower frequency bands require antennas to be placed at a high elevation for ideal transmission, the quarter wave height for 20 meters is 15 feet. This means the antenna can be attached to the eave of a house, hidden in an attic, or set up for field use with a few inexpensive tools, and it will allow you to communicate with people thousands of miles away.

Building an Antenna

Homemade antennas can be either resonant or non-resonant. One alternative to the end-fed design is the center-fed dipole. As the name implies, the feed point of this antenna is at the center of the radiating element. This is my favorite HF antenna to build. It requires only a few components. It's quick to set up and take down, and easily stored. To construct this antenna, we take the 33-foot-long wire required for 20 meters and cut it in half. This creates the two elements (each 16.5 feet in length) that are needed for a dipole. Because both elements are the same length, they are electrically balanced, meaning the impedance of one element matches the impedance of the other. Thus, a transformer is not needed because there is no impedance mismatch. A 1:1 balun can be used if a feed line is needed to connect the antenna to a radio. But for use in the field, a feed line and transformer are not needed.

I typically build this antenna from speaker wire, which can be purchased online or in most hardware stores. This may be considered a minor point, but it's worth mentioning here. The diameter of the antenna wire will affect the usable bandwidth that it provides. Bands such as 10 meters and 80 meters cover large segments of the radio spectrum. Thin wire provides suitable SWRs on a small segment of the radio spectrum. Thicker wire provides a bit more coverage. Narrow diameter wires like 24 and 26 gauge offer less bandwidth. If you want more bandwidth, consider using 14 or 12 gauge wire to build your antennas. I generally use 22 or 24 gauge wire for field antennas because it's light and compact.

If I want to operate on 20 meters, I know that I'll need two lengths of wire approximately 16.5 feet long. I also know I'm going to raise the antenna 15-20 feet in the air. I'll mark off 16.5 feet for the radiating elements with a pen on a roll of speaker wire. If my radio is 5 feet away from where the antenna wire will be located, I'll add 5 feet plus another 20 feet (the elevation of the wire) for a total of 25 feet. I'll add this to the total length of the speaker wire and cut it to that length. The excess speaker wire will be used in place of a feed line. I then separate the radiating elements, which are marked at the 16.5-foot mark, and leave the remainder of the wire unseparated. I wrap a bit of tape around the section of the wire where it splits to form the radiating elements to prevent it from splitting any further.

I connect the ends of each radiating element to a plastic s-shaped carabiner. These carabiners (available online) have different-sized holes along their sides. Antenna wires can be connected by passing them through a hole and tying an overhand knot large enough so that it doesn't pull back through the hole. I use a 10-15 foot length of paracord to fasten the carabiners to an attachment point (usually a metal camping stake pounded into the ground). Antennas emit a current of energy that can cause burns. It's essential to use an insulator at the end of an antenna wire to avoid grounding it or causing RF burns to a bystander or yourself. A plastic S-carabiner is an easy way to isolate the ends of the wire electrically, and it provides a handy attachment point. You can use other devices to secure the ends of the wire. Plastic S-carabiners are not necessary, but they make setup and take down easy.

One way to deploy this antenna is to use a multi-section painter's pole. As an alternative, Sotabeams makes a 19-foot (6 meter) telescoping carbon fiber mast that works well for temporary antenna deployment. To steady the painter's pole or antenna mast in a vertical position, a 5 gallon plastic bucket filled with sand can be used. A hole is cut in the lid of the bucket, large enough for the pole to barely go through. Using gaffer's or duct tape, locate the point where the separated speaker wires come together and tape that part of the wire to the top of the pole. **TIP:** When erecting a vertical mast for an antenna, consider securing it with stabilizing guy ropes that can be fashioned out of paracord. A metal hose clamp is fitted loosely around the mast with enough space for ropes to pass between the clamp and the mast. Three or four ropes are secured to it. If four ropes are used, one should be secured north of the pole, one to the west, one to the south, and one to the east. If three ropes are used, they should be positioned roughly 120 degrees apart. The ends of the ropes are tied to camping stakes driven into the ground. If you're concerned about the metal hose clamp damaging the surface of the mast, the hose clamp can be fed through a short length of rubber hose or the mast can be wrapped with electrical or duct tape.

At this point, I raise the painter's pole until the ends of the separated speaker wire are just off the ground. I pound a couple of aluminum camping stakes into the ground 15-20 feet from the base of the pole. Each radiating element (with its S-carabiner and paracord) is secured to its stake, leaving plenty of slack. I raise the painter's pole to the desired height. The ends of the radiating elements are now several feet off the ground. I adjust the length of the paracord to make sure that the radiating elements are tethered with a little slack in them to allow the speaker wire to move with the wind. When finished, I have an unseparated length of speaker wire going up to the top of the pole with the separated wires going downward in an inverted vee shape with the ends of the wires tethered to the ground.

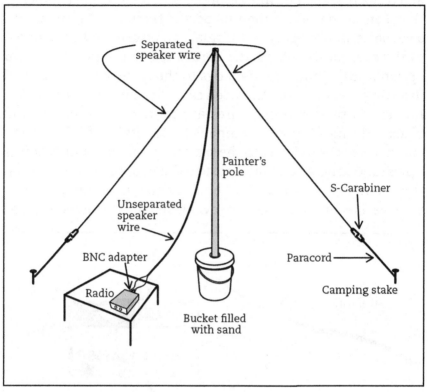

Speaker wire inverted vee antenna deployed with painter's pole

BNC Binding Post Adapter

As mentioned previously, a transformer and coaxial cable can be used to connect this antenna to a radio, but a BNC binding post adapter eliminates the need for both. A BNC binding post adapter (also known as a cobra head) is a small device used to connect antennas to radios. It has a BNC antenna port on one end and two threaded connection terminals on the other end. These adapters are available with either a male or female connector. (If your radio does not have a BNC antenna port, a separate adapter will be needed to use this device.)

To connect the antenna, split the unseparated speaker wire about five inches and strip the ends until an inch or two of bare wire is exposed. The wires can be connected directly to the red and black threaded terminals of the BNC binding post, which is then connected to the antenna port of the radio. Alternatively, a spade connector or ring terminal can be crimped or soldered to the ends of the wires and connected to the posts. A third option is attaching banana plugs to the ends of the wires and inserting them into the threaded caps that serve as receptacles. It does not matter which wires are connected to the red and black terminals if your antenna is horizontal. But if it is vertical, connect the red post to the radiating element, which points upward. Connect the black post to the counterpoise or radial that points downward. (BNC binding post adapters are inexpensive. I recommend having several on hand for emergencies.)

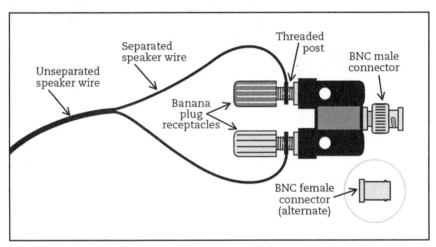

BNC binding post adapter with speaker wires connected

This antenna can be used as is, but it should be tuned for optimal performance. The 20 meter band goes from 14.000 to 14.350 MHz. The upper part of the band is used for voice transmissions. The lower part is used to transmit data signals. (Data modes are covered in another chapter). If you want to work data modes, try to tune the wire so the lowest SWR is at 14.175. For voice communication, shoot for 14.250 MHz. If the optimal SWR is *lower* than the desired frequency, the wires are too long. Trim them an inch at a time, checking the SWR each time you make a change. As you shorten the radiating elements, the lowest point in the dip on the SWR meter should move up in frequency. If the lowest SWR is *above* the desired frequency, the wires are too short. Lower the antenna to the ground. Locate the place where the unseparated wire begins and separate the wires a few more inches, and re-tape that section. Raise the antenna and recheck the SWR. Continue as needed until a satisfactory SWR is achieved. **TIP:** If you have a Nano VNA but aren't sure how to use it, many YouTube videos explain how to set it up, calibrate it, and take measurements.

What we have now is a 20 meter inverted vee antenna that will allow us to talk with people thousands of miles away, day or night. One point to consider is the slope of the radiating elements. Ideally, the two wires that form the inverted vee should be at 45-degree angles to the ground. Moving the ends of the wires closer to or further from the center support changes this angle, which alters the takeoff angle of radio waves. The 45-degree angle is not critical. Ten degrees, more or less, won't significantly affect performance. As the ends of the radiating elements are moved further away from the center support, the antenna begins to act more like a horizontal, which is still a usable configuration. However, one should avoid placing the radiating elements too close to the center support, as this may adversely affect performance.

25

Near Vertical Incidence Skywave and Ground Wave

WHEN A WIRE ANTENNA IS deployed at the recommended height of one-half wavelength above ground, a radio signal takes off toward the ionosphere at a low angle. A signal sent at a low angle skips off the ionosphere hundreds or thousands of miles away (depending on the frequency) and returns to the earth where it is received by a distant station. The area between the receiving and sending stations is called the *skip zone*. Receiving stations in the skip zone (ones that are close to the sending station) cannot receive the signal because it is directed skyward and passes above them. Only distant stations can receive the signal after it is directed back toward the Earth.

Half a wavelength for 80 meters is 40 meters. The recommended height for an 80 meter antenna is 130 feet above ground. Even at one quarter wavelength, it would be 65 feet above ground. For many people, that's an impractical height at which to deploy an antenna. What would happen if we deployed it at one tenth of a wavelength above ground? (For 80 meters, this would be roughly 25 feet.) When an antenna is deployed at a lower than recommended height, the signal takes off toward the ionosphere at a steep angle, typically between 80 and 90 degrees, depending on the frequency used and the antenna height. These nearly vertical signals skip off the ionosphere and return to earth within a few hundred miles of the sending station. If one needed to communicate with a friend or ally locally, as opposed to thousands of miles away, one could deploy an antenna at a lower than recommended height. The use of an antenna at a low height to make local contacts is called near vertical incidence skywave (NVIS). While antenna configurations for typical skywave use are directional, NVIS signals tend to be omnidirectional.

NVIS is best used on the 40, 60, 80 and 160 meter bands. It can be used to contact stations as close as one mile or as far as 300 miles away. The 40 and 60 meter bands are more usable during daylight hours, while the 80 and 160 meter bands are better at night. An antenna is typically deployed between 5-25 feet above ground in a horizontal configuration with the ends and center at the same height, or with the center a few feet higher than the ends.

There are many ways to set up an NVIS antenna. If you're looking for ideas, here's how I set up a 40 meter NVIS antenna:

For 40 meters, the total length of the radiating elements must be 20 meters for a half-wave dipole. You can position the feed point at the end of a 66 foot long (20 meter) wire and use a transformer. I prefer to place the feed point in the middle, which creates a balanced line and eliminates the need for a transformer. In this arrangement, two wires that are 33 feet long will be used. I cut two lengths of wire 35 feet long allowing two feet of extra length for tuning. I attach the far ends of the two radiating elements to 6 foot plastic garden stakes driven into the ground roughly 33 feet from the center support. (See diagram below,) As described previously with the 20 meter antenna, I use plastic S-carabiners and paracord to secure the ends of the radiating elements to the garden stakes.

A little creativity is used to build the feed point. Most BNC binding post adapters have two holes in them. I use a small (2 inch by 4 inch) sheet of 1/8 inch thick plastic that has holes drilled in it to match the holes in the binding post adapter. A zip tie is used to secure it to the sheet of plastic. Two more holes

1/4 inch in diameter are drilled near the edges of the plastic sheet toward one end. Plastic S-carabiners will be clipped through these holes. The near ends of the antenna wires are passed through the holes in two plastic S-carabiners and overhand knots are tied about two inches from the ends to prevent them from pulling back through. This provides strain relief so the wires are not pulled away from the terminals. The S-carabiners are clipped through the 1/4 inch holes in the plastic sheet. The ends of the wires are stripped and secured to the BNC binding post terminals. The plastic BNC mount is then secured to a garden stake, carbon fiber mast, or painter's pole with the antenna connector pointing downward. One end of the feed line is attached to the BNC connector. The other end is connected to a radio. Once the radiating elements have been trimmed to the optimal length, the NVIS antenna is ready for use.

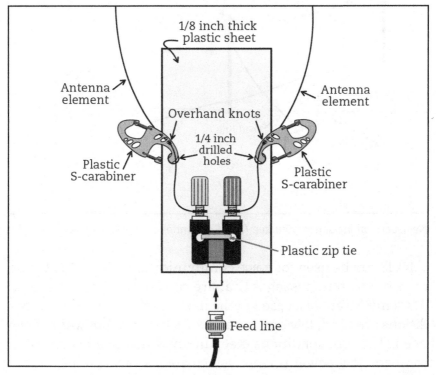

BNC binding post adapter secured to plastic sheet and connected to antenna

While a horizontal center-fed configuration is my preference for NVIS, an end-fed wire with a gentle slope will also work. An inverted vee, with the feed point higher than the ends is another option. **TIP:** For a stronger signal, wet the ground beneath the antenna. If you happen to have a pond or pool nearby, you can deploy the antenna near it, as water will help reflect the signal. (To avoid electric shock, do not to let the radiating elements come in direct contact with water while transmitting.) Another option is to cut a wire 5% longer than the radiating element. This wire is suspended below the radiating element or placed on the ground beneath it. The second wire acts as a reflecting element and should boost the signal.

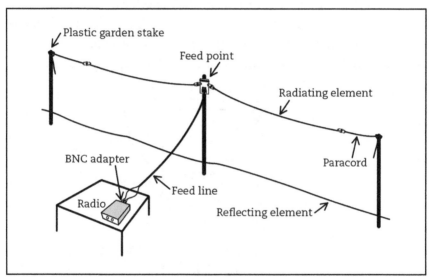

Near vertical incidence skywave (NVIS antenna)

NVIS can be used for voice communications as well as Morse code or written messages that are converted to data packets. (Data modes are discussed in the next chapter.) When band conditions are good, low power can be used, but full power may be needed in poor conditions. Keep in mind that in a hostile environment, low power transmissions are less likely to be discovered by an opponent using direction finding. With NVIS, signal strength and clarity are a mixed bag. Some stations will be difficult to hear (even when they are transmitting on 100 watts), while others may have strong signals when transmitting on low power. It's common for signals to change from weak to strong (signal fading) within a minute's time. **TIP:** If excessive noise is encountered, try lowering the antenna height. You'll receive a weaker signal, but it usually lowers the noise floor more than it reduces the signal. The result should be a better signal to noise ratio. If the local power grid is down, the man-made noise that normally makes it difficult to hear radio signals will be absent. Adjust your power setting and antenna height for the current operating conditions.

Ground Wave Signals

An alternative to sending skywave signals is using ground wave propagation. We know that UHF and VHF signals travel in a straight line while most HF signals travel skyward and reflect off the ionosphere. Ground waves are radio signals that travel parallel to the surface of the Earth, following its curvature up to several hundred miles beyond the horizon. Ground wave propagation is possible because low frequency waves are more strongly diffracted around obstacles. This allows them to continually bend downward to follow the Earth's curvature. Frequencies below 3 MHz use a mix of ground wave and skywave propagation. AM broadcast signals travel as ground waves during the day and skywaves at night.

During severe solar storms or any time when skywave propagation is out of the question, beyond the horizon transmission is possible with ground wave. Ground wave propagation requires the use of a vertical antenna and a low frequency band. The 160 meter band (frequencies between 1.8 and 2 MHz) is a good candidate. When urgent messages must be sent, remember that there are multiple ways to do it. Emergencies often require the use of unconventional tactics.

26

Data Modes

AS WE MENTIONED PREVIOUSLY, THE Meshtastic app allows users to send written messages over UHF radio. It does so by converting text to data and sending it by radio. In this chapter, we'll look at other ways to send written messages using HTs and HF radios. While voice communication is more natural, data transmissions use less bandwidth, less power, and in poor conditions, may be successfully transmitted when voice communication is impossible.

There are many ways to send information by data over radio. Typically, a program is used on a computer or phone that is connected to a radio by a cable or Bluetooth. The user composes a message on the phone or computer that has the appropriate software, which is then converted to a data packet, and transmitted via radio. It may be a difficult concept to grasp at first, but phones and computers can be used to communicate over great distances even when cellular networks and internet service are not available. Next, we'll discuss some of the most common data communication programs.

AndFlmsg

A handheld radio can send digitally encoded text messages or image files with the help of a phone or tablet using the AndFlmsg app. Text messages are composed in the app, which converts them to data packets, and sends them via RF. If the recipient also has the app and is on the air using the same frequency, they will receive the data packet, which will be decoded and translated as a text message.

A modem is used to encode and decode messages. Several modems are available for use in the AndFlmsg app. The modem is selected by the user in the modem settings tab on the app. Some modems are slower at decoding data, while others are faster. A few are overly sensitive to noise. I've had good success with the Olivia 4 125 modem. Image files can be sent using the MFSK modem.

The app decodes not just the signals it receives, but also any background noise. The trick is adjusting the squelch setting in the app so that it is just higher than the noise floor. That way, noise is filtered out and not decoded, while signals from other operators that break above the noise floor are decoded.

Here's how to do it. On the receiving tab near the bottom of the screen you'll see a yellow horizontal bar that represents the signal being received (including noise). The same bar shows the current squelch setting compared to the signal. Adjust the squelch level with the squelch up and down buttons until a signal received breaks just above the noise level shown on the bar. When set correctly, the app will only decode messages and not noise.

There are two ways to transmit a message with a phone and radio using AndFlmsg. The first way is to connect the radio to the phone with an APRS cable. (APRS is discussed below.) The second way is to use the built-in speakers and microphones of the radio and phone. With this method (known as audio coupling), a message is composed and sent on the phone while holding the radio nearby and pressing the push to talk button on the radio. The radio's microphone receives the audio signal from the phone and transmits it. On the receiving end, a similar process is used. The radio's speaker is held near the phone, which receives the transmission and converts it to text. Audible tones should be heard during transmission when using audio coupling. Anyone using the app who is on the same frequency and within range at that time will receive the message.

Encryption

In a hostile environment, you may want to encrypt your messages. Here are a couple of ways to do it: The AndFlmsg mobile app can send image files using the MFSK modem. Thus, it can be used with a steganography program that hides text or other files inside an image. Typically, a steganography app will prompt the user to open an image file. Then, text or another file is inserted into it and the final image is saved, and then sent. Some steganography programs offer encryption. Additionally, encryption is offered by several mobile apps that can encrypt text messages before they are sent. To send an encrypted text, compose it in the encryption app and then encrypt it. Copy and paste the encrypted message into the AndFlmsg app and send it.

Keep in mind that the sending and receiving parties must use the same app and have access to the encryption key to decode an encrypted message. The AndFlmsg app is not available through Google and Apple app stores. It must be downloaded from the web and manually installed. The app can be found on the SourceForge website on the Fldigi page. Look for the AndFlmsg.apk file. Although the FCC does not allow ham, FRS or GMRS operators to use encryption, it can be used on MURS and marine bands. If at a future date, the FCC loses its regulatory authority, encryption could be used on other bands.

Rattlegram

Handheld radios may be used with the Rattlegram app to send text messages transmitted as encoded data. Rattlegram works in nearly the same way as AndFlMsg, but only a single modem is used. Both sending and receiving parties must be on the air and on the same frequency when the message is sent. To use Rattlegram, compose a message in the app. Key the transmit button and hold the device near the radio while sending the text. A receiving station should have their phone near their radio to receive and decode the transmission. Anyone using the app who is on the same frequency at that time will receive the message, including a potential enemy. Encryption can be used on a band where it is not prohibited. **TIP:** Be sure both sending and receiving stations have the same version of the app installed to avoid problems.

APRS

Backpackers and other outdoor enthusiasts developed a way to send data packets over radio that includes vital information needed in an emergency. Automatic Packet Reporting System (APRS) is an amateur radio-based system for communicating real time information. Handheld radios are connected to a phone or tablet using an APRS cable or Bluetooth, and data is sent to listening stations within range. Data can include global positioning system (GPS) coordinates, text messages, and various announcements. APRS data is displayed on a map, which shows moving subjects, weather stations, and search and rescue data. If you are lost or in some other emergency and need immediate assistance, APRS is a good option. But because it transmits your position in real time, it presents a risk that must be considered if your situation requires a high level of operational security.

CAT Control

The data modes that follow are designed to allow a computer to control the functions of a radio. This arrangement is commonly called a computer aided transceiver, which is abbreviated CAT. The functions controlled by the computer include the selection of the operating mode and transmitting frequency. When a computer controls a transceiver, data operations run more smoothly. That said, it is not always possible or necessary to achieve CAT control. Although CAT control is desirable, most of the programs listed in this chapter can be used without allowing a computer to control the radio. When CAT control is not used, the operating mode and frequency are set manually by the user.

WSJTX

WSJTX is a program that converts written messages into data packets and sends them over a frequency determined by the user. WSJTX offers several modes of operation. FT8 is the most popular mode. It can be used to communicate with amateur radio operators around the world. Macros within the program allow sending and receiving of preprogrammed responses. Once a radio band is selected, FT8 automatically chooses the correct transmission mode and frequency and displays active users as colored rectangles on a waterfall display. Call signs of active users are displayed in a window. (A call sign is a unique set of numbers and letters that identifies a radio user.) Double clicking on a call sign will allow you to send a message to them.

Although FT8 is immensely popular, its use in an emergency is limited. It does not allow free text messaging and does not permit file transfers. It is however, an excellent tool for quickly determining what radio bands are usable. If a particular radio band is usable, when checking the most popular data mode in the world, there should be radio traffic on it. To determine what bands are in use, open WSJTX and select FT8 from the mode drop-down menu. On the waterfall display in the upper panel, as the program receives data, look for distinct colored markers indicating the transmissions of other users. High traffic as seen on the waterfall display indicates a usable band. Low or no traffic suggests the condition of that band is less than optimal. If you see signals from other users, it's likely you can make contact on that frequency (at least in the data part of the band). **TIP:** It can take several minutes for the waterfall display to show signals from other users. For faster identification of usable frequencies, note the notched waveforms on the bright green horizontal line at the bottom of the waterfall. This line is a graphic representation of signals on the frequency in real time. Each notch represents a transmission from a radio operator on the selected frequency.

When starting out as an amateur radio operator, you may want to know if your transmissions are being received by others and how far away you are being heard. One way to do that is with the WSJTX program in the Weak Signals Propagation Reporting (WSPR) mode. Signals sent in this mode are received and reported to a website that displays recent transmissions on a map. (This option requires you to enable reporting in the settings menu.) By logging into the wsprnet.org website, and entering your call sign in the search window, you can find out how far away your signals are being received. Checking your signal reports on the wsprnet.org website requires internet service. It's not much help when there is no internet service. But it's a useful for evaluating your radio and antenna when the internet is available.

JS8Call

JS8Call is a computer program that can be used to communicate with users around the world. If you prefer a simple program with only one mode, it's is good option. Once a radio band is selected, the program automatically chooses the correct mode and frequency on your radio and displays active users both on a waterfall and in a window. It can be used to send and receive scripted responses or spontaneously generated text messages. Some data programs allow the transfer of text, image, and other types of files. At the time of this writing, JS8Call does not permit file transfers. Messages sent on JS8Call (and all other programs) should be as short and concise as possible.

FLdigi (fldigi)

The grandfather of HF digital modes is fldigi. It can be used on all ham radio bands and it allows communication through several different modes. It supports both free text and preprogrammed responses, as well as file transfers and preformatted messaging. The user must choose the frequency, mode, transmission speed, and bandwidth to be used. The main program is fldigi, but other programs can be used with it to add functionality. Using flmsg, preformatted messages can be sent. Using flamp, files and images can be sent. When a particular individual must be contacted using a prearranged time, frequency, and mode, fldigi is a good choice.

Winlink

Winlink Express is a popular program that allows hams to send emails over radio. Messages can be sent on HF, VHF and UHF bands, either to a relay node or directly to another user. (A relay node is a radio station that passes messages between users.) In addition to sending emails to other hams via RF, messages can be sent to standard email addresses when the internet is available.

VarAC

VarAC combines the features of many of the programs listed above into a single application. It allows licensed amateur operators to send messages over radio in the open and through direct messaging. It also allows users to transfer files. Messages can be forwarded from station to station until the intended recipient is reached. Users can also set up group communication channels on specific frequencies.

Ion2G

Ion2G is a computer program that facilitates free-hand text messaging between HF amateur radio operators. The distinguishing feature of Ion2G is that it uses Automatic Link Establishment technology. The program quickly assesses conditions on all HF bands and automatically selects the best band for a particular user and tunes their radio to it when another station responds to their request.

As you can see, there are many options available for off grid radio communications. Knowing how to use them enhances one's ability to stay informed of current events. The best time to become familiar with these tools is before a crisis hits.

27

AREDN Mesh Network

AN OFF-GRID COMMUNICATION NETWORK CAN be built by connecting a few inexpensive network devices. A typical application of this concept is a large farm with several buildings where internet service is needed. Internet service at one building is sent via radio to other buildings. Each building is set up with a node that consists of a computer, a router board, and a radio transceiver. Data is sent from an internet hub to a computer. It is then sent to a router board using an ethernet cable. The router board sends data to the radio transceiver via ethernet cable, which beams it to another transceiver, which sends it to the router board at the distant station. The distant station's router board is connected to a computer, which allows users to access the internet.

Although this equipment is typically used to provide internet service, it can be used to create an off-grid communication network when the internet is unavailable.

The FCC allows amateur radio operators access to the UHF spectrum that is used by this equipment. Hams have designed a suite of programs under the name AREDN, which stands for Amateur Radio Emergency Data Network. AREDN software, when installed on computers, router boards, and radio transmitters, enables hams to communicate with each other over considerable distances without using the internet.

Because the equipment is designed to transfer large amounts of data, this type of network offers broadband capabilities, including video conference calling, voice chat, instant messaging, bulletin boards, phone calling by IP address, observation cameras, weather stations and more. Users can provide many of the services the internet offers, but it's all powered by radio.

A network is started by connecting two stations using a couple of radio transmitters, router boards, and computers. A third station can be added by connecting it by radio to one of the existing nodes. Each station that is added expands the range of the entire network. Fixed and portable nodes can be powered by household current, battery, or solar generator. Even if the power grid does down, the network can stay in service.

Many cities across the country have existing AREDN networks that ham operators can access. The AREDN website (arednmesh.org) has a map of existing nodes and pages where the software can be downloaded. The backbone of the Arizona Mesh Network (arizonamesh.org) is formed by two nodes located on mountains east and west of the city of Phoenix. Users connect via line of sight to one of the existing nodes, which connects them to other users on the network.

A variety of radio antennas are used and they can be divided into three categories. Some antennas are *omni-directional*. They transmit a signal in all directions. Others have a wide angle over which they can send and receive signals, typically between 45 and 120 degrees. These are called *sector* antennas. The third type is a *dish* antenna that receives and transmits over a very narrow angle typically between 5-7 degrees. These directional antennas offer higher gain and are used to communicate from point to point over longer distances.

As with all UHF radio operations, clear line of sight is critical for successful transmission of signals. UHF radio waves are easily blocked by tree foliage and buildings. Ideally, a node should be positioned at an elevated location. For temporary field operations, several antennas can be mounted on tripods within range of each other and powered by batteries. **TIP:** When setting up a communication plan that involves line of sight transmission of signals over considerable distance, find out first if there are any obstructions between sending and receiving stations. Several websites (including Google Earth) offer line of sight tools that are handy for this kind of work. To use them, locate your sending and receiving stations on the map provided, and the tool will tell you if there are any obstructions to line of sight between the two points. Some tools allow you to adjust the elevation of an antenna, if you plan to deploy it above ground level.

28

Communication Windows

WHEN PEOPLE COMMUNICATE BY RADIO, they are often strangers. Most radio hobbyists enjoy contacting people they've never met. Even in a crisis, it can be useful to contact a stranger. One party might need help that the other can provide. But there are times when you'll want to contact people you know via radio. That requires two people to be on the same radio frequency at the same time. Normally, you could email or text the other party and let them know you'd like to talk via radio at a certain time and on a particular frequency. How can you do this when internet and cellular services are disrupted? When normal communication is unavailable, we must plan prearranged times (windows), when parties know in advance to be on the air.

For a single communication event, two radio operators can agree to be on a certain frequency, using a certain mode at a certain time, for a given duration of time. This information can be communicated in person or by whatever other methods are available. For example, I might tell a friend when we meet in person on Tuesday that I will be on the air the following Sunday at 3:30 pm local time on 7.275 MHz using lower sideband for 15 minutes. If my friend is available, he can join me at that time. By planning a communication window in advance, we increase the probability of contacting someone intentionally. This single event could become a regularly scheduled on-air meeting or net.

If you wanted to build into your plan a few alternate times for communicating in case the agreed upon frequency is busy, or one party is not able to make contact at the arranged time, you might add other times, modes, and frequencies to the schedule. For example, I might tell my friend that in addition to the communication window described above, that on Sunday, at 8 pm local time, I will be on the 80 meter band using the JS8Call for 15 minutes. If desired, other communication windows can be added to the schedule.

Some preppers utilize a pre-scheduled matrix for emergency communication called the 3-3-3 plan.

Here is how it works:

- In a crisis, operators turn on their radio and listen for traffic at the top of the hour, every three hours for at least three minutes on channel 3.
- The preset hours are 3am, 6am, 9am, noon, 3pm, 6pm, 9pm and midnight.
- For non-amateur radio operators, channel 3 is CB-3, FRS-3, or MURS-3.

Since ham radios don't have channels, amateur operators would use one of the national calling frequencies such as 146.520 MHz FM simplex or another predetermined frequency.

If you need to contact specific individuals in a grid down situation, it's a good idea to develop a plan and explain it to all interested parties. Print out the prearranged frequencies, times, and modes, and keep them with other important documents.

29

Radio Reference Guide

THIS CHAPTER SUMMARIZES THE BEST radio options for communicating over a given geographic distance when phone and internet service are not available. Beginning at the neighborhood level and ending at global, radios suitable for each region are listed. Information is provided to indicate whether a radio transmits voice or text messages, if a particular type of antenna is needed, and when a license is required.

Neighborhood
- Nextel Direct Talk voice. No license required.
- FRS voice with handheld radio. No license required.
- MURS voice with handheld radio. No license required.
- Marine voice with handheld radio. No license required.
- GMRS voice with handheld radio. License required.
- FRS, MURS, marine, and GMRS radios may be used with the Andflmsg or Rattlegram app to send text messages.
- LoRa radio with Meshtastic app and phone or tablet. Encrypted text messages. No license required.

City
- AM/FM radio (listening only).
- MURS voice with handheld radio and Yagi antenna. No license required.

- Marine voice with handheld radio and Yagi antenna. No license required.
- GMRS voice with handheld radio and Yagi antenna. License required.
- Amateur UHF/VHF voice with handheld radio and Yagi antenna. License required.
- MURS, marine, GMRS, UHF and VHF amateur radios may be used with the Andflmsg or Rattlegram app to send text messages.
- LoRa radio with Meshtastic app and phone or tablet. Encrypted text messages. No license required.
- Amateur HF with NVIS antenna. Voice & data modes. License required.
- AREDN mesh network. License required.

County
- AM/FM radio (listening only).
- Marine voice with mobile radio. No license required.
- GMRS voice with mobile radio or repeater. License required.
- Amateur UHF/VHF voice with mobile radio or repeater. License required.
- GMRS, UHF and VHF amateur radios may be used with the Andflmsg or Rattlegram app to send text messages.
- LoRa radio with Meshtastic app and phone or tablet. Encrypted text messages. No license required.
- Amateur HF radio with NVIS antenna. Voice & data modes. License required.
- AREDN mesh network. License required.

State
- AM/FM radio (listening only).
- Amateur 2 meter band with Yagi antenna. License required.
- Amateur HF radio with NVIS antenna. Voice & data modes. License required.

Nationwide
- Shortwave radio (listening only).
- Amateur HF radio. Voice & data modes. License required.

Global
- Shortwave radio (listening only).
- Amateur HF radio. Voice & data modes. License required.

30

Getting on the Air

THERE ARE THREE HURDLES TO overcome if you'd like to become proficient in amateur radio operations. First, you must pass the license tests. Second, you must acquire some equipment, and third, you must learn how to use it. Josh Nass, who hosts the *Ham Radio Crash Course* YouTube channel has a video playlist that can prepare you for the amateur technician level test. Other YouTube channels have general and extra preparation videos. If you want to operate on HF, I suggest getting your technician license. As soon as you have it, get your general license. (Most testing facilities will allow you to take both tests on the same day.)

The FCC does not allow "broadcasting" on the radio bands described in this book. Strictly speaking, *broadcasting* is a one-way transmission where the receiving party cannot reply. Without a broadcast license, the FCC only allows transmissions between multiple parties.

It's good to get in the habit of listening to a radio frequency before transmitting. Listen for a full minute before transmitting to determine if anyone is using the frequency. If you transmit on a frequency that requires a license, you should receive a call sign from the regulating agency.

The usual way of finding a listening station in range of your radio is to request to make a contact with anyone listening.

If you're using a handheld radio this can be done by pressing the push to talk button on the side of the radio. Announce your call sign and ask if anyone is listening on the frequency. (On a radio with a microphone, depress the transmit button on the microphone.) If your call is KK7GSS, you would key the microphone and say, "This is KK7GSS, is anyone using the frequency?" The standard practice when calling a specific party is to identify the receiving party first and yourself second, i.e., "Hey you, this is me," or "WRTF695, this is KK7GSS" When someone responds, allow them to complete their message before replying.

In the U.S., licensed hams are required to announce their call sign at the end of a transmission and every 10 minutes during long transmissions. GMRS operators are required to identify themselves by call sign after a transmission and every 15 minutes thereafter.

Both voice and data transmissions can be done on UHF and VHF bands. FM is the most common mode used for voice transmissions. AM, digital and single sideband can be used, but they are less popular.

The most common HF mode for voice communication is single sideband (SSB). AM, FM, and digital voice modes are less popular. Single sideband is divided into upper and lower sideband. Generally, lower sideband (LSB) is used on frequencies below 10 MHz, while upper sideband (USB) is used for frequencies above 10 MHz. Morse code uses a mode called CW, which stands for continuous wave.

The jargon used by HF operators includes a variety of two and three letter codes referred to as Q codes. When you want to start a new conversation on HF, you *call CQ*. It might sound like this: "CQ, CQ, CQ... KK7GSS calling CQ." Remember to listen for other operators before transmitting. When a ham operator hears you, they might reply by stating your call sign and adding "QSL," which is an acknowledgment that your transmission was heard.

Unique cultures are found in each radio community. Citizen Band radio operators use jargon that's different from the language used in amateur radio. UHF hams use different terminology than HF amateurs. Each has its own way in which users are expected to operate. If you don't want to be corrected by others for using incorrect etiquette, learn the culture of the community before transmitting.

One way to become familiar with radio etiquette is to listen to or participate in regularly held on air meetings called *nets*. A net is an on-air meeting that is scheduled at the same time of day and on the same frequency, usually on a weekly basis. Many local amateur radio clubs hold weekly nets where anyone who is licensed can participate. Newbies can ask questions and get answers from experienced hams. Weekly nets are hosted on UHF, VHF and HF frequencies. An internet search can help you find a net your area.

Whether weekly nets would be on the air in a grid-down crisis would depend on whether the hosts have access to backup power. For VHF and UHF nets that rely on repeaters, it would depend on whether the repeaters have back up power. If you find nets of interest, consider printing out the dates, times, and frequencies and keeping them with other important documents.

Another regularly scheduled activity on HF is *contesting*. Typically held on weekends, some amateur bands are filled with operators who try to make as many contacts as possible during a set time period. If you want to learn the etiquette of amateur radio, one way to do it is to listen to or participate in contests.

Radio communication skills take time to develop and they diminish over time. If you want to become proficient, set aside a few minutes a week to practice them.

31

Communication Security

THE INFORMATION IN THIS BOOK is primarily intended for those who will communicate off-grid in a friendly environment. However, there may arise a need to operate in a hostile environment—one where an adversary intends to harm you or negate your ability to send messages. The collection, analysis, and exploitation of communication is the realm of signals intelligence (SIGINT). This chapter will briefly address the issue of communications security, or COMSEC.

The average person cares little about communication security. They email friends and send text messages to relatives without worrying about who might receive those messages aside from the intended recipient. Ham radio operators seldom worry about their transmissions being intercepted by an adversary. During times of peace, there is little direct threat to our safety from the messages we send. During times of civil unrest or war, our messages may be of great interest to an adversary, who views us as a threat. Such an individual may gather information about our plans based on our communication signals.

Whether between ex-lovers on social media, or armed combatants during war, the communications of an opponent can be used against them. I've found that refraining from making frequent personal statements on social media is a wise tactic. It gives potential opponents little ammunition to use against me. That same principle can be used to safeguard yourself against an opponent seeking to exploit your electronic communication during a time of chaos.

Soldiers who fought in Afghanistan employed a set of intelligence gathering tactics to locate opponents and eliminate them. The first step was to identify a potential target inside an area of operation. This was often done by listening for radio signals, which was the most common way Afghan militants communicated. Once a transmission was heard, soldiers continually monitored transmissions on that frequency. Radio direction finding techniques were used to pinpoint the physical location of the sender. Troops would then observe the individual or group and make notes about their daily habits, building a pattern of life. Once enough information had been gathered, it would be exploited.

Signals intelligence gathering is not the exclusive domain of the government. Anyone equipped with a few inexpensive devices can collect radio and phone signals and use them against an adversary.

Here are some guidelines for operating safely in a hostile environment. The first consideration is preparing to send a message. Limit your transmissions to only those messages that are absolutely necessary. Know why you are getting on the air and know exactly what your message must be. Write out your message in advance. Edit the message so that it conveys the exact information required in the fewest words possible. When you transmit, be as brief as possible. Try to keep your transmissions to less than five seconds.

Take steps that make it difficult to understand your message. Encode or encrypt messages when possible. Use digital modes as well as analog. Instead of using single sideband on HF, consider transmitting on AM or FM. On VHF, instead of transmitting as most people do on FM, use single sideband. (Remember that when using a handheld radio, the FM mode typically requires an antenna to be in a vertical position, while single sideband uses the antenna in a horizontal position. It's okay to reverse this practice for the purposes of COMSEC, but be sure that the intended receiving party is aware of the antenna orientation you're using.)

The next consideration is avoiding practices that create a predictable pattern of behavior. Avoid transmitting repeatedly on the same frequency. Consider transmitting on one frequency and receiving on another. Use multiple bands, such as VHF marine, UHF 70 centimeter and HF 40 meters, all of which can be used locally. Avoid transmitting at the same time of day or the same day of the week. If you're communicating with an individual or team, this will require you to develop a communication plan with preset times, frequencies, and modes.

In a grid-down situation, using low power will conserve batteries, but it will also make your signal harder to detect by an opponent. Use the lowest power setting needed to get your message through. Use directional antennas like the Yagi, which make direction finding more difficult. Although the Meshtastic app and a LoRa radio are a good option for a friendly environment, they rely on a phone or tablet and radio which continually transmit metadata identifying you and your location, making you an easy target.

Situational awareness is critical to survival when operating in a hostile environment. Habits that are acceptable in peacetime can get you killed or captured during times of war. Know your environment at all times. Know which practices are safe and which are not. If you'd like more information about communication security and operating in a hostile environment, NC Scout has a series of books (listed below) that cover these issues in greater depth.

The Guerrilla's Guide To The Baofeng Radio
The Guerrilla Dispatch: Volume 1
The Guerrilla's Guide to Signals Intelligence

32

How God's Kingdom Responds to Crisis

THIS IS WHERE A TYPICAL book on preparedness might
end. But this is not a typical book on preparedness. What sets
this book apart from others on the subject is my belief that the
supernatural power of God should be considered when making
plans to survive a crisis. I believe that if you're prepared spiritually, the need for expensive, time-consuming preparations
may be lessened. Someone who is spiritually prepared will fare
much better in a crisis than someone who is not.

During a crisis, it's tempting to adopt a "me against them"
attitude toward society. If you've prepared for an emergency
and others haven't, you'll be tempted to lock the unprepared
masses out of your home and let them fend for themselves. No
one would blame you. But God may have a different plan. When
Jesus was followed by a hungry crowd, the disciples' solution
was to send them away and let them get their own food. Jesus
responded by telling the disciples to give them something to eat.
The disciples reacted with incredulity. But a few minutes later,
they handed out enough food to feed 5,000 people with baskets
left over. God's kingdom responds to lack with abundance.

During a food shortage, you are going to be approached by
hungry people. One response is to turn them away. But you
could offer them what you have, trusting that God will increase
your supply and allow you to feed even more people.

God has led me to teach others about miracles of healing, food multiplication, and other manifestations of His kingdom. This is an unconventional way to prepare for a crisis. But when you consider that God can provide a supernatural solution to any problem, why would we overlook this option? The most important question is whether we are trained and equipped to manifest God's goodness.

Many people have chosen not to prepare for times of crisis, preferring to pin their hopes on the goodness of God. They believe that in times of dire need, He will sovereignly rescue them from harm. This saves them the time and expense of having to prepare. More often than not, such divine rescues don't materialize. There are reasons why this is so. As an example, let's look at divine healing.

Most Christians have been taught that divine healing comes when we ask God to heal someone. We pray, and God hears our prayers. Based on His knowledge of the situation, He decides whether to heal them. Most people who embrace this model seldom see anyone healed. This approach is not the way healing is demonstrated in the New Testament.

If you carefully examine the lives of Jesus and the disciples, you may notice something strikingly different about their approach to the miraculous. Healing the sick, the working of miracles, and raising the dead were not things they did occasionally. They were a part of their daily lives. By watching Jesus, the disciples learned how to respond to every crisis the way sons of God are supposed to respond. When an unexpected storm blew in, Jesus taught them to rebuke it. When a family member became ill, He taught them to heal the sickness. When there was not enough food, He taught them to multiply what little they had. He even taught them how to walk on water. Day after day, through His sermons and actions, He taught them that the normal response to a problem for one of His disciples was to release something from God's kingdom into the situation. The response to sickness was healing, the response to death was resurrection, the response to lack was multiplication, and the response to a storm was to calm it. This is what the life of a disciple should look like.

No one can possibly prepare for every conceivable crisis. You can (and should) prepare for medical emergencies. But if you come across someone whose illness is beyond your ability to manage and you can't transport them to a hospital, what are your options? A disciple of Jesus can release power to heal them. You can store a supply of food, but if bread is unavailable, you can pray over your last loaf and watch it feed your neighborhood. This is how God would have us live—both in times of peace and times of crisis. Our resources are limited but God's are not. A common-sense approach is to prepare to the best of our ability and believe that God will provide what we do not have. That requires a heart that wants to provide for others as well as ourselves.

Divine Healing

A few people begged Jesus for healing, but the Lord never asked His Father to heal anyone, nor did the disciples. Jesus and the disciples did not ask God to heal the sick because they had received the power and authority to do it themselves.

Then He called His twelve disciples together and gave them power and authority over all demons, and to cure diseases. He sent them to preach the kingdom of God and to heal the sick.
LUKE 9:1-2

Jesus and the disciples healed entire villages. Unfortunately, the life of the average Christian looks nothing like this. Few of us are releasing miracles the way the disciples did. Most of us can only hope that God hears our prayers. A few years ago, I didn't believe in divine healing. After shedding my unbelief and renewing my mind to the truth, I began seeing people healed by the dozens.

The authority to heal and the power to work miracles comes from being a disciple of Jesus. If you're not His disciple, you should become one. Ask Him to come into your life and the

Spirit of God will come and reside in you. Then you will have the power and authority He gives to all His disciples.

Working miracles and healing the sick is done by faith. It's that simple. If you believe with absolute certainty that when you pray for a sick person, they are going to be healed—they will be healed. When they are healed, you'll know your faith is pure. If they aren't healed, you'll know your faith needs strengthening.

Children often have great success in healing because they haven't been poisoned by doubt. Their faith tends to be pure. If you have doubts about God's desire to heal the sick, ridding your mind of doubt is essential. One way to build faith for miracles is to pray for anyone who will let you. At first, you may not see many people healed, but eventually you will. I had to overcome a lot of doubt when I first attempted divine healing. It took months before I saw anyone healed. As I prayed with more people, my faith grew, and the frequency of miracles increased. You can expect the same results.

Here are some tips to help you become more effective in healing. If you need healing, find someone to do it. My own healing made a profound impact on my faith to heal others. I suffered for months with aggravating shoulder pain. One day, I went to a meeting where a man prayed for me. At the time that he prayed, I felt nothing. It wasn't until 24 hours later that I felt the pain leave, and realized that I was healed. Pursue your healing until you receive it.

Read books on healing and miracles, and watch videos—especially testimonies and instruction. Many people who operate in healing have podcasts. I have healing resources on my website prayingmedic.com.

Like every other kind of prepping, healing won't happen if you never get started. Pray for anyone who will let you—friends, family, co-workers and strangers. When I'm out in public, I look for people with canes, casts, immobilizers, splints, wheelchairs, and people hobbling along in obvious pain. These people are usually open to healing. Start by introducing yourself. Engage the individual in small talk. Build some trust, and ask if you can help them by getting them healed. If they say no, bless them and keep going.

You'll find different methods of healing. Most of them work. Some are better than others. But none are foolproof. I saw an approach that I liked. I borrowed it and adapted it to fit my personality. It works for me, but it doesn't work for everyone. Don't get hung up on following a certain method. Develop your own style. You might consider using different methods at different times. Jesus used a different method nearly every time He healed someone and had great success.

Among my friends who have the highest success rates in healing, there is agreement on one approach that seems to work best. It involves commanding sickness or pain to leave and commanding healing to take its place.

If you're able to physically touch the sick person, it may help, but it isn't necessary. In many cases, I'm not able to touch the one I'm praying for and they're still healed. Command sickness, disease, inflammation, pain, depression, and unclean spirits to leave. Next command organs, blood vessels, nerves, ligaments, tendons, bones, discs, cartilage, muscles and other anatomical structures to be healed.

Many forms of illness are related to demons. Evil spirits should be told to leave using the authority Jesus gives us. (It isn't necessary to raise your voice when commanding demons to leave.) I've had experiences where I commanded a knee or ankle to be healed and nothing happened even after five or six attempts. In some cases, I closed my eyes and God showed me a demon that needed to be removed and in other cases, I assumed a spirit was there and commanded it to leave. In almost every case, the next command brought complete healing. If healing is going poorly, consider the possibility that a demon is present that must be removed.

Don't be discouraged if nothing happens the first time you command healing to happen. Ask the person if you can pray again. Don't be discouraged if nothing happens the second time. Do it again. Don't give up if nothing happens the third time. Do it again. Keep commanding the problem to leave and command the sick or injured body part to be healed. You'll have to get used to a little embarrassment. You may look a little foolish repeatedly commanding a broken leg to be healed when there's no outward sign that it's helping. Yet most healings I've seen came because I stood there looking like an idiot, repeatedly commanding an injury to be healed until it finally was healed. When I started seeing people healed, most of it came after four or five times of commanding healing to happen. Be sensitive to the wishes of the one you are trying to heal. If you have permission to continue, be persistent and don't quit. If you see any change in symptoms or severity of pain after four or five times, keep going. You're making progress. If you see any change at all, you can eventually get the condition to go away completely.

I don't recommend starting with an infirmity that feels too big for your faith. Joint injuries like strains and sprains are relatively easy to heal. When you are new, praying for these injuries is a good way to build faith. As you see people healed, and as your faith grows, you should look for opportunities to pray for people with more serious conditions.

In the practice of healing, patience is worth its weight in gold. Some people will be healed after an hour of battling against the illness. Would your time be well spent if it took two hours to get someone healed of diabetes or blindness? Would you consider it a good use of your time if it took 15 hours to get someone healed of Lou Gehrig's disease? Would you be content to pray for a resurrection for 24 hours if that's what it took? As your faith grows, healing will take less time, and the frequency of miracles should increase.

Calming the Storm

When Jesus calmed the storm on the Sea of Galilee, He demonstrated the kind of authority that is given to the children of God. He challenged His disciples to stop limiting themselves and pursue greater miracles than they thought possible. He said to them:

"Most assuredly, I say to you, he who believes in Me, the works that I do he will do also; and greater works than these he will do, because I go to My Father."
JOHN 14:12

Jesus is our role model. We know about the miracles He worked from the Bible. He wants us to do those same miraculous works. He has given us the power and authority we need to do them. As God's representatives, we have authority not just over demons and sickness but over natural disasters. During the last ten years, I've witnessed countless miracles including sudden changes in the weather after commanding an approaching storm to be calm. Exercising authority over the weather takes a bit of practice, but in time, it can become a normal response to a storm. In the aftermath of a nuclear war, you might command toxic debris to become harmless. Since Dr. Mendoza recommends not running the heating or air conditioning for two weeks after a nuclear detonation, you might command the weather to change so that you don't need to run your air conditioning or furnace.

Gas Tank Miracles and Food Multiplication

Many of the testimonies I've heard are from friends who have driven hundreds of miles with a nearly empty tank of gas. These gas tank miracles happen when a person has unshakable faith that their car will keep running, regardless of how much gas is in the tank. I've heard many testimonies of food multiplication as well. This typically happens when a meal is prepared for a certain number of guests and more people show up to the meal than were expected. Those in charge of preparing the food simply declare that the food will not run out and there will be plenty for all with some left over. In most cases, the food is multiplied as it is served—just like when the disciples fed the multitudes with a few loaves of bread and fish. Some people have prayed over their pantries and had boxes of food materialize supernaturally.

Supernatural Repair of Broken Machines

Preparedness would be much simpler if we didn't have to worry about repairing broken machines. During times of crisis, spare parts will become scarce and finding an honest repairman may be difficult. While it's good to have tools and parts on hand for some of the more commonly needed repairs, I'd like to share the following story to illustrate the fact that God has a way of fixing broken machines that doesn't require you to store spare parts or acquire technical knowledge.

In 2012, I bought a used car for my daughter that had a lot of miles on it. The engine had been hesitating and occasionally stalling at intersections. When my daughter moved out of state, we didn't need it anymore, but I didn't want to sell it in that condition. I wouldn't get a fair price for it. So, I thought I'd change the spark plugs and fuel filter in the hope that I could getting it running better before selling it. If it ran without hesitating, I might get a little more money for it.

On my way out to the garage to work on the car, the Holy Spirit reminded me of a previous miracle where a broken machine was repaired supernaturally.

As I walked to the tool box, I thought, why not? If He did it before, He can do it again.

I got inside the car, closed the door, and made declarations that the ignition system would work properly and the fuel system would be cleaned out.

"Come on, Angels! Get to work on this car and make it run, in Jesus' name!"

I prayed over the car and made declarations for three or four minutes. Then, I turned the key and drove it down the street. At the first intersection, it accelerated smoothly. It hadn't done that in six months. I drove it for about ten minutes, through many intersections. At some intersections, I felt fear creep into my mind. I wondered what I would do if it started to hesitate. Sure enough, the car hesitated when I became fearful. So, I commanded the car to be healed and kept driving. I dealt with my fear by imagining the car accelerating smoothly through each intersection. Each time I did this, there was no hesitation in the engine.

I drove home and told my wife what happened. She didn't believe me. So, we went for a drive. The car drove perfectly and never hesitated once. We listed the car and sold it for a few hundred dollars more than we paid for it. The people who bought it test drove it and remarked at how nicely it ran. They were delighted to take it off our hands.

If you're prone to believing that you're on your own in a crisis and that God won't help, you may want to reconsider your understanding of His ways. He cares about our problems and wants to fix them in ways that bring Him glory. Sure, you can pay someone to fix your broken car, but if you cooperate with God, and He repairs it supernaturally, you'll have a testimony to share with the world.

I believe that when power grids fail and neighborhoods are dark, a few houses will be powered by God's supernatural kingdom. I expect that when no one in town has cellular service, some will send text messages on the Holy Spirit's cellular network. If cars run out of gas and mass transit is unavailable, God can transport us supernaturally to any location. And if an area is hit by an EMP, some will pray and have their radios and cars restored to working order. God is not limited by the conditions imposed by the physical world.

Preparedness takes on a different meaning when you see it from the perspective of God's kingdom. Jesus said it was our responsibility to pray that the will of God would be done on earth as it is in heaven. As ambassadors of God's kingdom, we are here to enforce His will on earth in the same way it is enforced in heaven. Since there is no sickness in heaven, we're responsible for eradicating sickness on earth. Since there is no lack in heaven, we're responsible for bringing the abundance of heaven to earth. Transferring the resources of heaven to earth is the responsibility of every believer, especially during a crisis.

If you're not working miracles during times of peace, you have a slim chance of doing so during a crisis. Miracles are released through faith. In times of crisis, fear tends to increase. Fear destroys faith, and with it, the manifestation of the miraculous. It's easier to have faith for miracles during peace time than during a crisis. The time to grow our faith for miracles is now.

Other books from Praying Medic

For up-to-date titles go to: PrayingMedic.com

Series—The Kingdom of God Made Simple:

Divine Healing Made Simple
Seeing in the Spirit Made Simple
Hearing God's Voice Made Simple
Traveling in the Spirit Made Simple
Dream Interpretation Made Simple
Power and Authority Made Simple
Emotional Healing Made Simple

Series—My Craziest Adventures with God:

My Craziest Adventures with God - Volume 1
My Craziest Adventures with God - Volume 2

Series—The Courts of Heaven:

Defeating Your Adversary in the Court of Heaven
Operating in the Court of Angels

And more:

Emotional Healing in 3 Easy Steps
The Gates of Shiloh (a novel)
God Speaks: Perspectives on Hearing God's Voice (28 authors)
A Kingdom View of Economic Collapse (eBook only)
American Sniper: Lessons in Spiritual Warfare (eBook only)

SCAN THIS TO GO TO
PrayingMedic.com

7/9/2024

Lt. Mark Brennan USMC Ret.
(Logistican & Planner)
Commanders Intent — a method
- Purpose = Prepping
- Method = overview
- End State = awareness
choose to go further
Situation [method]
Vulnerabilities

- JIT = Just In Time Logistics = no stockpiles
- Lack of Toughness
- Pandemic etc.
What to do? A way to prepare + approach the problem
- mental, physical, logistics to thrive
  - Survive
[Reconnection/method] - assist others in societal collapse

1) Identify requirements + acquire needed logistics
2) Plan + coordinate w/ other like minded
3) Develop rugged + resilient mindset to prepare for adversity
4) Seek God's Direction by Prayer

End State

1) Secured water sources
2) Supplies on hand to sustain
3) Shelters readied
   Defenses prepared
4) Plans in place to assist
5) Min. 30 days supplies / stores "

Planning Considerations
1) Water, Matches
2) Food - rice, beans, seeds, p. butter
3) Shelter
4) Defense/groups, Community
   o medical expertise

hickey
Collapse of systemic portions
in our our societal systems

— Criminals
— Vandals
— Shortages   Opportunistic
                Random

Beyour
own 911   Violence   Confrontational
                                      Antifa, BLM, LGBQT
                                      antisemetic Insurgents
Protectionist   Preplanned
— Citizens   Terrorists
— militias   Direct action
3rd   Insurgent groups
appt   — Terror cells
groups   usp?   non state actors

DETAILS

12 million border crossings since '21

Who are they?
n.A. Insurgency Syndicate

Revolutionary + insurgency groups
in U.S. recognized, have an
organizational hierarchy + whose
stated goals are to topple the existing
social order.
Exercising our consciences.
STRATEGY
- Seduce
- Scare
- Subdue
- Silence

How? why What?
(NOT)
Who What When Where How

The Playbook

n Ai's

Religion "FATWA" = Religious
decree

Killing up to 1 mil. US children

TO
govern
a
Divorce
is
coming?

Destroy

Influence

Islamic
MARXISM

cognitive
Dissonance

2 counter
movements
- one seeks to
influence govt
the other seeks
to destroy

Action Plan

TRUST

1. E.R. Make an E.R. plan

1 gal/water per person per day for 3 weeks

- most likely contingencies
  - what do you need to support family.

- Develop alternate courses of action

- — This is my family's E.R. plan

Communication
- no phones
- alternatives
- Tech + Nontech

Coordination
1) Know your neighbors
2) Inform & organize network
3) Practice the skills — Tradecraft
   ~~Techniques~~ + procedures (de-evolution of)

The situation always dictates
- Be flexible
- no plan survives 1st contact

A. Bug Out Bag — get out quickly   3-7 days survival
B. get Home Bag — phone ER contacts
C. Shelter in Place ≠ 3 weeks

TOP 3) Scenarios (7-8 min.)

① Break of law enforcement & emergency response (EMS)

② The grid goes down

③ Supply chain shortages

GHB

phone
ER contacts

Flashlight
Pocket knife
Lighter
mask/Respirator
Li-ion rechargeable battery pack
- weatherproof notepad + pen
- small self defense weapon

handgun,
Pepper spray
ASP
stungun